After Walden

LEO STOLLER

After Walden

Thoreau's Changing Views on Economic Man

"Is there any such thing as wisdom
not applied to life?"
HENRY DAVID THOREAU

STANFORD UNIVERSITY PRESS · STANFORD, CALIFORNIA

Stanford University Press
[1966, c 1957] Stanford, California

© 1957 by the Board of Trustees of the
Leland Stanford Junior University

Printed in the United States of America
Original edition 1957
Reprinted 1966

Published with the assistance of
the Ford Foundation

TO

Louis T. Friedman

PREFACE

This book, as its title indicates, is a study of one aspect of a complex man, and that for only one part of his life. It was begun in the doctoral seminar of Professor Ralph L. Rusk at Columbia University, interrupted, resumed in New York on an Advanced Graduate Fellowship of the American Council of Learned Societies, interrupted once again, and finished at Wayne State University, in Detroit. That it was completed at all is owing in large part to the aid, encouragement, and patience of the ACLS, of Professor Rusk, of Professor Lewis Leary, and of Professors Joseph Dorfman, Joseph Blau, Oscar James Campbell, Emery Neff, and Frank Davidson. What other debt I owe to my wife and children all will understand who have themselves experienced the itinerant years in the life of an English teacher.

Parts of the first and fourth chapters appeared in the *New England Quarterly*.

Leo Stoller

Wayne State University
Detroit, Michigan
September 1957

CONTENTS

After Walden

1

Dissociation of Opposites

Henry Thoreau is the man who lived alone in a hut by Walden Pond and went to jail rather than pay taxes. Such, at any rate, is the thumbnail sketch of him by an America eager to tolerate what it considers primitivism and oddity. But Thoreau abandoned his hut and spent fifteen years, most of them intensely active, in sociable Concord. And instead of resigning from government all that time, he became an advocate of social legislation and supported the Union in its war with secession and slavery. Moving to the pond and going to jail had been thoughtful solutions to serious problems. When they turned out to be ineffectual, Thoreau went ahead to look for others. This search is the subject of our book.

It was an earlier quest, which we shall only glance at, that yielded the decision to farm a small plot and to live alone on it in a house of his own building. Thoreau had come home from Harvard College in 1837, age twenty, to a situation whose analogue was to be experienced by graduates almost a century later. America was entering a major depression. Each person had his unique problem to solve, his own paths to choose among. But to the men and women called reformers the predicaments of the individual and of the nation seemed inseparable. Working from different axioms, they suggested a whole prism of ways out, unpragmatic ways such as religious perfection and ideal communities and the abolition of money. They published their theories chiefly in New York and Boston and preached them everywhere, including Concord, where they sought the ear and the pen of Waldo Emerson. It was among these thinkers that young Thoreau moved, looking for his own way out. "Men are constantly dinging in my ears their fair theories and plausible solutions of the universe," he wrote in his journal in 1838, "but ever there is no help, and I return again to my shoreless, islandless ocean, and fathom unceasingly for a bottom that will hold an anchor, that it may not drag" (VII, 54).[1]

The product of Thoreau's intellectual sounding was an outlook not unlike that of the other reformers. Its ideal was self-culture: life aimed at full realization of every man's and woman's innate capacities. Its embodiment was to be in one man standing opposed to the industrial order. But when Thoreau came to test this theory at Walden Pond, he found its major elements incompatible with two areas of actuality: the America to which they were being applied, and the aspect of his personality which spontaneously responded to this America. It was this incompatibility that returned him to Concord, to a maturity radically different from the youth of which the life by the pond had been the climax.

I

The immediate antecedent of Thoreau's ideal appears to have been the self-culture preached by the Unitarians and especially by William Ellery Channing. Channing transmitted to a later and a different age the faith in human perfectibility which he had learned of the Enlightenment. "Let us not disparage that nature which is common to all men," he declared, "for no thought can measure its grandeur. It is the image of God, the image even of his infinity . . . no limits can be set to its unfolding." He subsumed the whole virtue of individual life under the ideal of an integral perfection, in striving toward which "all the principles of our nature grow at once by joint, harmonious action, just as all parts of the plant are unfolded together."[2]

The devotion of young Henry Thoreau to this ideal of self-culture

---

[1] All references in this form are to *The Writings of Henry David Thoreau* (20 vols., Boston and New York, 1906).

[2] *The Works of William E. Channing, D.D.* (Boston, 1875), pp. 13, 15.

is amply attested by his writings. Elements of the doctrine are to be found scattered through the fragmentary journals of the late thirties and early forties, and a complete statement, as we shall see later, is in his early essay "The Service." But in adopting Channing's ideal, Thoreau grafted it onto an economic stock of anti-industrialism and onto a theory of social action suited to his own temperament.

Thoreau's opposition to industrial society was already well established in 1839, when he and his older brother took the trip on the rivers whose incidents make the framework of his first book. Rowing down the sluggish Concord, they came before long to its juncture with the energetic, cascading Merrimack. Look up this "sparkling stream to its source," wrote Thoreau, "and behold a city on each successive plateau, a busy colony of human beaver around every fall. Not to mention Newburyport and Haverhill, see Lawrence, and Lowell, and Nashua, and Manchester, and Concord, gleaming one above the other" (I, 89). Here the early industrialists had raised their gray stone mills on the edges of the river. Proud of their life work, these provincial giants boasted of it even in architecture, proclaiming in rigid, honest, and unadorned lines the straightforwardness of their search for profit. Thoreau and his brother rowed past these impassive but eloquent structures as quickly as possible, anxious to escape their contamination and reach the purity of the untouched forests in the north. They did indeed stop long enough to investigate meadow-bordered Salmon Brook and "learn its piscatorial history from a haymaker on its banks" (I, 167), but a mile and a half further upstream the mouth of the Nashua was "obstructed by falls and factories" and did not tempt them to explore it (I, 169). At Manchester too they made haste "to get past the village here collected, and out of hearing of the hammer which was laying the foundation of another Lowell on the banks" (I, 260).

It seemed to Thoreau that the factory system, erecting a new world before his eyes, operated against the interests of both nature and man. In rhetoric which captures, if it also exaggerates, the violence that was one element in his temperament, he championed the shad whose passage upstream was blocked by factory dams, exclaiming, "I for one am with thee, and who knows what may avail a crowbar against that Billerica dam?" (I, 36) More calmly he declared later: "I cannot believe that our factory system is the best mode by which men may get their clothing. The condition of the operatives is becoming every day more like that of the English; and it cannot be wondered at, since, as far as I have heard or observed, the principal object is, not that mankind may be well and honestly clad, but, unquestionably, that the corporations may be enriched" (II, 29).

The persistence of this rejection of industrialism ultimately led Thoreau to seek a way of practicing self-culture outside the accepted social order. But during the years when he was turning such an alternative over in his mind, he tested the method suggested by Channing and his adherents for men whose jobs could not add to their development. It premised that self-culture, being an individual matter, was possible despite the social system of machines and profit, and its key was the disciplined exploitation of spare time. Thus Frederic Henry Hedge, proclaiming that "the work of life" is "the perfect unfolding of our individual nature," went on to say that since the business of society "is not the highest culture, but the greatest comfort," the best which the aspirant might get from it was to be let alone after work. He must "expect nothing from Society, but may deem himself happy, if for the day-labor, which necessity imposes, Society will give him his hire, and beyond that leave him free to follow his proper calling, which he must either pursue," Hedge ironically concluded, "with exclusive devotion, or wholly abandon."[3]

Testing this advice, Thoreau became increasingly convinced of an incompatibility between self-culture and a profit-centered civilization. In the eight years between his graduation from Harvard and his removal to the pond he sought in vain for an occupation which would not conflict with the activities that yielded his poems and essays. He tried pencil making, school teaching, magazine writing, odd-jobbing. He turned to reform, after this, with a resolution that paralleled the desperation he remarked in his townsmen.

Pencil making was the occupation of his father, a dry goods clerk in Concord early in the century, later a storekeeper and farmer and day laborer moving from place to place in Maine and eastern Massachusetts, and finally, when Thoreau was about six, in Concord again,

---

[3] " The Art of Life—the Scholar's Calling," *Dial,* I (October 1840), 171–7 .

manufacturing square-leaded pencils that were a good article but got him little wealth. Thoreau very likely helped out in the shop behind the house as soon as he was old enough, and as late as 1836, a junior at Harvard, he was peddling pencils with his father in New York (XIV, 66). College made a new occupation possible. Thoreau was already teaching school during vacation, and after his graduation he turned to the classroom for a livelihood. He taught for more than three years, all in Concord: in the town school, in a private school in his own home, and in the Academy which he had himself attended. Then, early in 1841, done with teaching and out of a job, he tried to buy a farm, found he hadn't enough money, and turned to odd jobs. One April day he earned seventy-five cents "heaving manure out of a pen," and though he told himself in his journal that "great thoughts hallow any labor" (VII, 250 f.), he did not turn down Waldo Emerson's invitation to enter his house as general handy man. Thoreau remained financially dependent on Emerson in one way or another for three years, first in Concord and then, for most of 1843, in the Staten Island home of brother William Emerson, whose young son he tutored in exchange for room and board and enough cash to cover expenses while he tried to break into the New York magazines. He failed both as tutor and journalist. "Literature comes to a poor market here," he wrote to his patron at the end of the summer (VI, 107), and more plainly to his mother, "My bait will not tempt the rats,—they are too well fed" (VI, 108). In the end he returned to Concord and to the pencil shop.

These early efforts of Thoreau to earn a living (whose details our review is not concerned with) are of three sorts. In one he tries to support himself by writing, the activity central to his own self-culture. In the second he works at a job indifferent to the economy: teaching. In the third his occupations bring him directly into acquisitive society and subject him to its pressures.

It was certainly prerequisite to the Walden experiment that young Thoreau should not make money from his poems and essays. But his commercial failure as a writer must not be estimated grossly. His lack of success was not an inability to attain goals shared with others; his adherence to reform does not smack of sour grapes. Perhaps it was as inevitable that his writings should not sell as that his policy of not punishing pupils should be frowned on by the school board. He taught in the Concord public school for two weeks without flogging, and then one old member of the board informed him that such teaching could not succeed; Thoreau used his ruler on six children chosen at random and resigned the post. His bedrock radicalism was bound to crop out in what convention would deem failures.

In earning a living, Thoreau would not betray the practice of self-culture, what he called his own business, and this made the choice of an occupation a matter of principle rather than of expediency. He stopped being a teacher because he not only had to dress the part but to "think and believe" accordingly (II, 77), and he had learned that the thinking of a schoolmaster and the thinking of an artist were not complementary. When he returned to Concord early in 1844 from his venture with the New York publishers, he worked for a while at pencil making and made certain improvements in the graphite mixture that promised commercial success. But as he says in *Walden*, he not only "found that it would take ten years to get under way" but that he would probably be on his way "to the devil" (II, 77). No division of his day between lower and higher aims seemed possible. In the years that preceded his removal to Walden Pond, Thoreau saw himself being drawn into the pit which had already engulfed his neighbors, whose lives were wasted in seeking wealth or in earning a living.

Concord was economically rusticated, a backwater town relatively free of the evils of industrialism then becoming evident in other areas of New England. But Thoreau, penetrating deeply into this small world, found the souls of his townsmen encrusted and enslaved, their potential freedom perverted into desperation.

He learned that the laboring man, striving to maintain the market value of his hands and brain, had "no time to be anything but a machine" (II, 6). He found society devoted to ends which made it inevitable that some do "all the exchange work with the oxen, or, in other words, become the slaves of the strongest" (II, 63). After the smoke of the railroad is blown away, he declared, "it will be perceived that a few are riding, but the rest are run over" (II, 59). For "we do not ride on the railroad; it rides upon us," and each of the sleepers that tie the tracks is a man. "The rails are laid on them, and they are covered with sand, and the cars run smoothly over them (II, 102 f.). With unusual penetration, he summed up the treadmill life of the small tradesman: "always on the limits, trying to get into business and trying to get out of debt, a very ancient slough, called by the Latins *aes alienum*, another's brass, for some of their coins were made of brass; still living, and dying, and buried by this other's brass; always promising to pay, promising to pay, to-morrow, and dying to-day, insolvent; seeking to curry favor, to get custom, by how many modes, only not state-prison offences; lying, flattering, voting, contracting yourselves into a nutshell of civility, or dilating into an atmosphere of thin and vaporous generosity, that you may persuade your neighbor to let you make his shoes, or his hat, or his coat, or his carriage, or import his groceries for him; making yourselves sick, that you may lay up something against a sick day, something to be tucked away in an old chest, or in a stocking behind the plastering, or, more safely, in the brick bank; no matter where, no matter how much or how little" (II, 7 f.).

Seeking to avoid for himself the fate of his fellows and to discover a way by which all men might labor toward perfection, Thoreau looked for a social order which would not reduce men to animals and machines but would be consistent with the devoted pursuit of self-culture. In this search he was one among many. All about him in those late thirties and early forties were men and women driven by the utopian impulse, trying to remodel acquisitive society or to anchor a noble dream outside it. There were fetishists of the person, who believed in some single discipline practiced by the individual on himself—eating only fruits and vegetables, drinking only milk and water, preparing for the end of the world due to arrive next April or, failing that, next October; and there were fetishists of society, who believed in the family-sized farm, in the phalanstery, in this or that preconceived ideal arrangement by which to work and to eat and to sleep. They were men and women whose conscience, as Parrington said of one of them, had "slipped its leash of the practical."[4]

Living as he did in Concord, the suburban headquarters of re-

---

[4] Vernon L. Parrington, *Main Currents in American Thought* (3 vols. in 1; New York, n.d.), II, 345.

form, and making excursions to its metropolitan centers in New York and Boston, Thoreau personally met representatives of all its arguments. To the Concord Lyceum, which he had probably joined while still preparing for college, came speakers on all subjects of the day. And into the Emerson household trooped every variety of reformer, the well-known and the anonymous. One day in Manhattan Thoreau talked with the pacifist Henry C. Wright, the Fourierist Albert Brisbane, and the eclectic reformer William Henry Channing (VI, 81). There too, at Emerson's request, he looked up Edward Palmer, "the man without & against money,"[5] who had for several years been advocating the abolition of currency and who was now also studying with an herb doctor and associating with a circle of mystics. A few weeks before Thoreau talked with him, Palmer had issued a leaflet headed "Herald of Holiness," proclaiming himself a new John the Baptist commissioned to announce the imminent coming of perfect individuals to redeem the race.[6]

But to categorize and sample these reformers are beyond the limits of our glance at Thoreau's early search. One point only must be insisted on. Differing though they all did on methods, they often joined on ideals. When Brook Farm, for example, was being organized, Thoreau exclaimed in his journal, "As for these communities, I think I had rather keep bachelor's hall in hell than go to board in heaven" (VII, 227). But its leading spirit, George Ripley, hoped equally with Thoreau for a new world in which mankind might practice self-culture successfully. The "great object of all social reform," he wrote, is "the development of humanity, the substitution of a race of free, noble, holy men and women, instead of the dwarfish and mutilated specimens which now cover the earth."[7] And neither man provided a place in his utopia for the relationship of employer and wage earner or for the conflicts associated with the existence of social classes. The prescriptions of the utopian experimenters become in the end merely curious: it is only their ideals that can remain meaningful.

---

[5] Ralph L. Rusk, ed., *The Letters of Ralph Waldo Emerson* (6 vols.; New York, 1939), II, 170.

[6] Reprinted in *Pathfinder,* I (April 22, 1843), 141.

[7] John T. Codn a *Brook Farm; Historic and Personal Memoirs* (Boston, 1894), 147 f.

Thoreau's own method of reform was wholly individualistic and tinged with practices derived from the fetishists of the person. Like his contemporaries, he prescribed life for an abstract human nature. But having rejected the forms of economic activity presented him by industrial society, he first had to go "outside" society to discover a new economy adequate to his conception of man. Hence it was that Thoreau believed it would be "some advantage to live a primitive and frontier life" and thus "learn what are the gross necessaries of life and what methods have been taken to obtain them" (II, 12). The "improvements of ages" seemed to him to have had "but little influence on the essential laws of man's existence" (II, 13), and it was to get at these laws that he wished "to front only the essential facts of life," "to live deep and suck out all the marrow of life," "to drive life into a corner, and reduce it to its lowest terms" (II, 100 f.).

In a parallel way he sought to arrive at the essence of man's requirements by removing the many wrappings with which history had covered him and laying bare the primal man as he had existed in "the old dawn of time, when a solid and blooming health reigned and every deed was simple and heroic" (VII, 134). For the young Thoreau the period before the invention of the plow was one of original perfection from which society had progressively degenerated (VII, 454). In what was perhaps a moment of unusually dogmatic adherence to this view of history, he wrote that "war and slavery, with many other institutions and even the best existing governments" were to be considered "the abortive rudiments of nobler institutions such as distinguish man in his savage and half-civilized state" (VII, 16 n.). Obvious concomitants of this primitivism were idealization of the American Indian and high praise for the heroes of Ossian, in whom Thoreau discovered civilized men reduced to essentials. "They stand on the heath," he wrote, "between the stars and the earth, shrunk to the bones and sinews."[8]

But what Thoreau found, or thought he found, by the recovery of absolute human nature was an economic order whose idealization was already a commonplace of his day. Its basis is quickly illustrated in the description left by an early New Englander of a situation

---

[8] "Homer, Ossian, Chaucer," *Dial*, IV (January 1844), 293.

which seemed to him "the most favorable to social happiness of any which this world can afford." The economic unit of this "happy society" was "a town consisting of a due mixture of hills, valleys and streams of water: The land well fenced and cultivated; the roads and bridges in good repair; a decent inn for the refreshment of travellers, and for public entertainments; The inhabitants mostly husbandmen; their wives and daughters domestic manufacturers; a suitable proportion of handicraft workmen, and two or three traders; a physician and lawyer, each of whom should have a farm for his support."[9] Writing before the end of the eighteenth century in a region that approximated his own conception, Jeremy Belknap shut out of his economy of freeholders and mechanics both the slaves and plantation owners of the South and the entrepreneurs and wage earners of the new industry that was even then crossing the Atlantic. But he accepted the necessity of commerce, and its place though subordinate was respectable. It was this happy Jeffersonian society that was the foundation of Thoreau's utopia.

Not unexpectedly, however, in an idealization no longer supported by an actual way of life, Thoreau's projected economy was one which even Belknap could never have witnessed. In the period of the trip on the rivers, for example, his social ideal was still close enough to its Jeffersonian antecedent to provide an honorable place for commerce. Thus a passage of *A Week on the Concord and Merrimack Rivers* celebrating the life of the Merrimack River boatmen includes the following verses:

> Ships with the noontide weigh,
> And glide before its ray
> To some retired bay,
> Their haunt,
> Whence, under tropic sun,
> Again they run,
> Bearing gum Senegal and Tragicant.
> For this was ocean meant,
> For this the sun was sent,
> And moon was lent,
> And winds in distant caverns pent. (I, 224 f.)

---

[9] Jeremy Belknap, *The History of New Hampshire* (3 vols.; Dover, New Hampshire, 1821), III, 251 (first published in 1792).

But this approval of commerce is already mixed with the opposite attitude that is before long to replace it. The journal for 1841 denounces the phrase "he is doing a good business" as "more prophane than cursing and swearing" and indicative of a "blasphemous" way of viewing things. "There is death and sin in such words," Thoreau exclaims. "Let not the children hear them" (VII, 251). By 1851 he had for some time been convinced that "trade curses everything it handles; and though you trade in messages from heaven, the whole curse of trade attaches to the business" (VIII, 319 f.).

It seemed to Thoreau that the "complex" way of earning a living (as he was later to call it) introduced between a man and the goods and services he actually needed a whole series of unnecessary intermediate activities. The farmer is poor, he wrote in *Walden,* because he is "endeavoring to solve the problem of a livelihood by a formula more complicated than the problem itself. To get his shoestrings he speculates in herds of cattle" (II, 36). What Thoreau was suggesting was that as far as possible the farmer make his own shoestrings, weave his own cloth, grow his own food, and build his own house. "Who knows," he asked, "but if men constructed their dwellings with their own hands, and provided food for themselves and families simply and honestly enough, the poetic faculty would be universally developed, as birds universally sing when they are so engaged?" (II, 50.) At the pond Thoreau had built his own house and believed that he had demonstrated that he could "avoid all trade and barter" in obtaining his food (II, 71). And like him, he thought, "every New Englander might easily raise all his own breadstuffs in this land of rye and Indian corn, and not depend on distant and fluctuating markets for them" (II, 70).

Such an economy practiced with consistency, whether by an isolated person or by a whole nation, entailed a low level of productivity which could never satisfy the demand for goods and services characteristic of a more advanced system. Intimately associated, therefore, with Thoreau's ideal subsistence unit was a rigorous asceticism. The farmer "would need to cultivate only a few rods of ground" and would find it cheaper to spade it himself than to employ draught animals—provided he would "live simply and eat only the crop which he raised, and raise no more than he ate, and not exchange it for an insufficient quantity of more luxurious and expensive things" (II, 61). Just as the "complex" industrial and commercial economy was to be restored to the "simplicity" of a more primitive agricultural era, so each man's life was to be reduced to essentials, that the energy hitherto wasted on superfluities might contribute to the soul's perfection. "Simplify, simplify," he directed. "Instead of three meals a day, if it be necessary, eat but one; instead of a hundred dishes, five; and reduce other things in proportion (II, 102).

Thoreau's own asceticism extended beyond the point required by opposition to the acquisitive ideal. There seems to have been present in him even as a young man a certain repugnance for the physical in human beings. He did indeed once write, almost in the words to be used by Walt Whitman, "Good for the body is the work of the body, good for the soul the work of the soul, and good for either the work of the other" (VII, 174). But he also wrote that "the body is the first proselyte the Soul makes," that "our life is but the Soul made known by its fruits, the body," and that "the whole duty of man may be expressed in one line,—Make to yourself a perfect body" (VII, 147), and one suspects that he was not accepting the work of the body but talking rather of a process of control and what might be called purification. Thoreau's list of "divine suggestions . . . addressed to the mind and not to the body," which continues with "not to buy or sell or barter" and concludes with a few reticent etceteras, begins with "not to eat meat" (VII, 382).

Nor was this attitude of his the result of a merely intellectual acceptance of such doctrines as vegetarianism. In 1852, looking back upon his earlier years, he wrote that he had "rarely for many years used animal food, or tea, or coffee, etc., not so much because of any ill effects which I had traced to them,—as because they were not agreeable to my imagination" (II, 237). It seemed to him that "the repugnance to animal food is not the effect of experience, but is an instinct" (X, 417). The economic aspect of his social program, like its theory of action to be discussed later, was thus in keeping with the truth of his own personality; but a distinction must be drawn between the minimum essential to the program and the excess essential to the man.

Behind the asceticism and behind the atomistic society of handicrafts and subsistence agriculture was the ideal of a life all integral,

whose every activity would help ripen the unique product lying potential in the soul. "The whole duty of life," he had once written, "is
contained in the question how to respire and aspire both at once"
(VII, 300). In his vision the labor which supported the body, by being also an end in itself—"industry . . . its own wages" (VII, 157)—
would simultaneously enlarge the soul.

His favorite way of giving this difficult concept expression was
through the image of time and eternity. The man who does not
aspire to perfection and labors only to maintain his body or to ac-
cumulate wealth works within the limits of a time which is external
to him. Since his soul marches in place, his life shows no true sequence, and his actions "do not use time independently, as the bud
does," which helps "lead the circle of the seasons" (VII, 215). The
aspirant man whose labor contributes steadily to his perfection creates
his own time, which has nothing in common with ordinary time,
but is a sequence established by incremental activity against the background of eternity. "As time is measured by the lapse of ideas, we may
grow of our own force," he wrote, "as the mussel adds new circles to
its shell" (VII, 206). The achievement of the "artist in the city of
Kouroo" who devoted his entire life to making a walking stick was
that by striving after perfection in his manual task he overcame the
contradiction between time and eternity and did not age but continued to develop and become more nearly perfect in a perennial
youth (II, 359 f.).

Whatever its metaphysical overlay and however unpragmatic its
proposed embodiment, here is an ancient ideal of mankind, often
frustrated and as often expressed again: the liberation of man from
the everlasting pecking after corn which denies his mind full freedom,
and the elevation of the labor imposed as a necessity by nature to an
artistic activity which will discipline the spirit.

II

An economic program based on a return to the soil is not in-
trinsically associated with any form of social action. For the agrarian
it may mean political parties, newspapers, and agitation for a Homestead Law. For the communitarian it may involve soliciting capital
from a wealthy supporter, enlisting recruits, and buying a large farm.

For Henry Thoreau it meant creating in his own life and with only his own resources a veritable microcosm of the ideal social order to serve as a model for mankind.

The rationale behind this program is best examined in Thoreau's essay "The Service," completed sometime in 1840. Here, in imagery derived from art, light, spheres, and sound, Thoreau has embodied the whole of his early transcendentalism, which strove to perfect mankind by centering earth on the single man and urging him on to a correspondence with the goodness of the enveloping oversoul.

This oversoul of transcendentalism may be likened to the mind of an artist, freed, however, of the deficiencies which keep most human thought from perfection. The artist conceives his work and then executes it; whatever change he makes in the medium is first a change in his thought. And his mind does not stand still. As it moves onward, it conceives and executes new works. But there is a lag between conception and execution while the imperfect hand labors to reproduce the perfect thought. If, therefore, a painting were endowed with a striving for perfection, it would want to overcome this lag and bring itself into true correspondence with the image in the mind of the painter. This is to assume, of course, that the artist's mind is moving of itself and that the artistic act can have no effect on the mind which conceives it. So indeed did the transcendentalist assume that the oversoul moved of itself and was altogether independent of its products. As the oversoul moved, it put forth man and the natural world about him. Nature, being without individuality, might thus be read as its representative. Man, however, was both its product and its imperfect instrument: being possessed of will, he could follow patterns different from the perfect ones made perceptible in his soul. The only duty, therefore, of the man who sought perfection was that of "yielding incessantly to all the impulses of the soul"[10] and in this way developing the innate potentialities which would keep him in correspondence with deity. It was this, in the largest sense, that Thoreau meant by self-culture.

The whole duty of man—workman, thinker, artist—was to perfect his own unique self: "every stroke of the chisel," proclaimed young

---

[10] *The Service,* ed. F. B. Sanborn (Boston, 1902), p. 1.

Thoreau, "must enter our own flesh and bone." Moreover, it was the entire man who was to be perfected, not some single aspect of the character whose development would be at the expense of the rest. The "coward," the man who does not aspire to correspondence with the oversoul, is "wretchedly spheroidal at best, too much educated or drawn out on one side, and depressed on the other," but the "brave man" is "a perfect sphere," concentric, as it were, with the great sphere of the oversoul. To the revolutions of this great sphere—that is, to the higher law—each man must attune his life, till it becomes "a stately march to an unheard music."[11]

Through the individual man thus perfected, the inherent goodness of the oversoul then reaches those others whose souls remain servants of will. At times the successful aspirant seems a kind of skylight through which effulgence pours in upon us—for if only a "single ray" penetrate our atmosphere, writes Thoreau, "it will go on diffusing itself without limit till it enlighten the world." More often the imagery suggests an invincible solipsistic energy, the creativity of the oversoul transferred to the perfected man. Bravery becomes "a staying at home and compelling alliances in all directions." Having heard celestial music, the brave man "compels concord everywhere, by the universality and tunefulness of his soul."[12]

The peculiarity of this complex of ideas is that it sanctions a program of social action which demands no action upon society. Opposing the ideals of life usually associated with utilitarianism, it nevertheless commands its practitioner to seek his own ends—provided they are just—and to leave the accountancy of the moral arithmetic to heaven. Such "individual reform" as distinct from "social reform" was a central tenet of young Thoreau's social philosophy. On one of the work sheets of an early and still unpublished lecture, he demanded that the reformer who recommends a new "institution or system" be certain that he "represents one perfect institution in himself—the centre and circumference of all others—an erect man." "I ask of all reformers," he continued, "of all who are recommending temperance—justice—charity—peace—the family—community—or associative life—not to give us their theory and wisdom only—for

---

[11] *Ibid.,* pp. 24, 6, 15. [12] *Ibid.,* pp. 8, 1, 15.

these are no proofs—but to carry around with them each a small specimen of his own manufactures—and to despair of ever recommending any thing of which a small sample at least cannot be exhibited.—That the temperance man let me know the savor of temperance, if it be good—the just man permit me to enjoy the blessings of liberty while with him—the Community man allow me to taste the sweets of the community life in his society—that I may know what his large promises mean." The legacies of the great benefactors of mankind, he pointed out, had not been manuals to direct our actions, but their own biographies.[13] These heroic individuals who embodied their teachings in their own lives had given way, however, to mere preachers. "There are nowadays professors of philosophy," he wrote in *Walden*, "but not philosophers." For to be a philosopher is "so to love wisdom as to live according to its dictates," that is, "to solve some of the problems of life, not only theoretically, but practically" (II, 16).

Thoreau's determination to act out all his principles was central to his greatness both as man and writer. For although the organic theory of literature in which he believed cannot account for his mastery of language, its conviction "that poetry itself is an organic outgrowth of the poet's character"[14] freed him to undertake the actions that provided some of his best work with content.

At the same time there was a limit never altogether removed from this determination: that his responsibility ended when he had embodied the principle in himself. To become a squatter by the side of Walden Pond and there attempt to demonstrate the practicability of a subsistence economy as the foundation for self-culture was enough. If other men observed his success or listened to his descriptions of it and were convinced by his example, they were then free to follow.

This limitation, too, had its effect on his writing. For although he could write excellent paragraphs of cold, incisive prose laying bare

---

[13] Ms. Am. 278.5 in the Houghton Library of Harvard University, by whose permission it is here quoted.

[14] Fred W. Lorch, "Thoreau and the Organic Principle in Poetry," PMLA, LIII (March 1938), 297.

the inhumanity of the social order, the young Thoreau left no significant body of criticism to document his aversion to industrial and
commercial America. Believing as he did in the efficacy of individual
perfection to reform society, he preferred to write of his own cure
rather than of others' illnesses. His very first published article, on
the Latin poet Persius, maintained that "satire will not be sung," that
the poet "had best let bad take care of itself, and have to do only with
what is beyond suspicion." "If you light on the least vestige of truth,"
that is of goodness, he continued, "an eternity will not suffice to extol
it, while no evil is so huge, but you grudge to bestow on it a moment
of hate." Proper satire will not be describing evils but be free of
them: "the divinest poem, or the life of a great man, is the severest
satire."[15] Thus oriented, Thoreau deprived himself of the extra-
ordinary power to capture the particular which was perhaps his out-
standing quality, and by reducing the direct representation of evil in
his writings on society gave disproportionate emphasis to a certain
nagging tone whose implied smugness offends many readers.

The best example of this paradoxical theory of social action, which
limited the action to that of the individual on himself, is in young
Thoreau's belief that his greatest contribution to the defeat of slavery
would be to refuse to pay his poll tax to the State of Massachusetts.
Thoreau had begun withholding his tax before he removed to the
pond, but a fortunate accident of history postponed his arrest until the
second summer of his experiment, reminding us of the perfect con-
gruence between the economy established at Walden and the politics
with which it was associated.

Thoreau was confident that only the perfectionist atomistic unit
which aspiration had led him to create "outside" society gave the
fullest freedom to attack slavery. Those who had not detached themselves as he had might "speak of moving society," but they had "no
resting-place without it" (IV, 384), nothing immovable on which to
stand and no fulcrum on which to rest the lever that was to dislodge
the evil. Self-interest of one kind or another kept them back. "Practically speaking," he wrote, "the opponents to a reform in Massa-

---

[15] "Aulus Persius Flaccus," *Dial,* I (July 1840), 117 f.

chusetts are not a hundred thousand politicians at the South, but a hundred thousand merchants and farmers here, who are more interested in commerce and agriculture than they are in humanity, and are not prepared to do justice to the slave and to Mexico, *cost what it may*" (IV, 362). The stake in the social order which was a consequence of being within it rather than outside not only tied the North economically to the South but prevented the antislavery Northerner from opposing the political state which tolerated the existence of slavery. For the rich man "is always sold to the institution which makes him rich," and whoever pursues wealth rather than self-perfection "cannot spare the protection of the existing government" (IV, 372 f.). To be free of the economic consequences of opposing the State, a man must "hire or squat somewhere, and raise but a small crop, and eat that soon" (IV, 373). Thoreau's own ideal economy would purge a man of all material interest in society and enable him to execute unhindered the behests of the oversoul. And it was unquestioning obedience to the higher law which would overthrow evil. "Action from principle," he declared, "the perception and the performance of right, changes things and relations; it is essentially revolutionary, and does not consist wholly with anything that was" (IV, 367).

Having thus based opposition to slavery on withdrawal from the economy of the North, Thoreau sidestepped the problem whose solution is the marrow of democratic political strategy: how to achieve that union with expediency by which principle can gain popular support. It was not his task to convince Northern farmers and entrepreneurs and wage earners that their long-term self-interest demanded abolition, but to show how a man who sought to live his own life by principle might satisfy the oversoul on the question of slavery.

Consistent with the premise that the absolute goodness of the oversoul is to be embodied microcosmically in the life of the single person, Thoreau's suggested action was first of all wholly individualistic. The extent of his commitment to individualism in politics is perhaps best evidenced in his review of the abolitionist newspaper *Herald of Freedom*, printed in the *Dial* a year before he moved to the pond.

This newspaper was issued in New Hampshire by Nathaniel Peabody Rogers,[16] a reformer whose individualism would not bear the least trespass upon its integrity. Rogers tells us that he sought "an ever-changing—advancing—improving—learning—never stopping—undefinable position," as much position as might be found in "a charging army," and whatever clogged his independent advance he strained to shake off. The free speech he championed had for its motto "no committees—nor commitment" and left no room even for the chairman of what he called a "corporate" meeting. His rules of order were "the order of human nature" and his parliamentary manual "every body's own bosom." Here is his description of a satisfactory antislavery society: "Association—but of associate individuals—whole individuals—unabated and undiluted. Concert of action—but of individual, personal action—where no combination can bring upon individual freedom, the wizard spell of the majority—where that monstrosity is not known—where unfelt and unacknowledged, is the influence of numbers and the authority of names—where are no great men—no leaders; that sends out its great truths backed up by no external or intrinsic force, to make their own way to the free and unawed hearts of the people."[17]

George Ripley, whose communitarian views might elsewhere have diluted his truth, did not err in saying that Rogers "carried the principle of individualism to an intensity of heat that threatened to consume every form of organization by which men are bound together in social relations."[18]

By 1844, Rogers' form of individualism, called "no organization" among the abolitionists, had apparently been an issue in Middlesex County (of which Concord is a township) for several years. At a convention of the county Anti-Slavery Society in April 1841, Garrison himself had been present to introduce resolutions, later adopted, stating that "no organization (as now advocated in certain quarters)"

---

[16] Robert Adams, "Nathaniel Peabody Rogers: 1794–1846," *New England Quarterly,* XX (September 1947), 365–76; Wendell P. Glick, "Thoreau and the 'Herald of Freedom,'" *ibid.,* XXII (June 1949), 193–204.

[17] *A Collection from the Newspaper Writings of Nathaniel Peabody Rogers* (Concord, New Hampshire, 1847), pp. 344, 380, 308, 293, 380.

[18] *Harbinger,* VI (November 6, 1847), 4.

was "unphilosophical and pernicious in its tendencies" and that "so long as slavery continues in this land, in an organized form, so long are we persuaded that an organized opposition to it will be essential to its overthrow."[19] Whether any part of Concord was understood to be specifically included within those "certain quarters" we do not know, but it is significant that when the Thoreau brothers made their trip on the rivers in 1839 they stopped off to visit Rogers,[20] and that when the inevitable collision between Rogers and the organized Garrisonian abolitionists came in 1844, Thoreau thrust himself publicly into the controversy with his review.

The brief review merely hints at the true issue (the ostensible one was ownership of the *Herald of Freedom*) in the remark that no other newspaper "asserted so faithfully and ingenuously the largest liberty in all things." For the rest it praises Rogers as a stylist, finding "more unpledged poetry in his prose than in the verses of many an accepted rhymer," and acclaims him as a reformer whose position is "honorable and manly"—that is to say, who fits Thoreau's conception of what a reformer ought to be: a man whose "feet were still where they should be, on the turf," and who "looked out from a serener natural life into the turbid arena of politics" (IV, 306 f.).

When Rogers received his copy of the *Dial*, he immediately made use of Thoreau's review to defend himself against the charge of the organized Garrisonians that the quality of the *Herald* had begun to fall.[21] But no defense against peripheral accusations could have headed off the defeat that seemed in the nature of things to be awaiting the doctrine of no-organization. Rogers was forced out of his editorship, and his kind of extreme individualism ceased to be significant among the abolitionists. But it lingered on in various

---

[19] *Liberator*, XI (April 30, 1841), 71.

[20] Thoreau refers to this visit in a short unpublished manuscript about Rogers written sometime after the posthumous publication of Rogers' *Newspaper Writings* and apparently meant for inclusion in *A Week*. This manuscript now forms part of Ms. Am. 278.5 in the Houghton Library of Harvard University, by whose permission it is here referred to. F. B. Sanborn mentions this visit in *The Life of Henry David Thoreau* (Boston and New York, 1917), p. 228.

[21] Glick, "Thoreau and the 'Herald of Freedom,'" p. 199.

persons, among whom was Henry Thoreau, who remained to the end a "come-outer," independent of all reform organizations.

In addition to being wholly individualistic, Thoreau's suggested antislavery action was to demonstrate that his own perfectionist microcosm was a free world. His problem being to embody truth and then let it speak for itself, his task was not to address himself to the slave-owning in others but to the slave-owning in himself. "Only *his* vote can hasten the abolition of slavery," he declared, "who asserts his own freedom by his vote" (IV, 364). He had not come into the world to make it "a good place to live in, but to live in it" (IV, 368), and he had his own high goals to attend to. But as his goal was to perfect his own soul, he must demonstrate that he was free of evil within by making certain that he did not give any sanction to evil outside himself. A man need not "devote himself to the eradication of any, even the most enormous wrong," he wrote, "but it is his duty, at least, to wash his hands of it, and, if he gives it no thought longer, not to give it practically his support" (IV, 365).

Such support was being given to the evil institution of slavery, Thoreau believed, by any person who in any way supported the governments of Massachusetts and the United States. For it was the government of the United States whose Constitution sanctioned the existence of slavery and which was even then waging an unjust war against Mexico, and it was the government of Massachusetts which by its membership in the Union supported the Constitution and which was about to send its troops to support this war for the extension of slavery. "How does it become a man to behave toward this American government today?" asked Thoreau. "I answer," he wrote, "that he cannot without disgrace be associated with it. I cannot for an instant recognize that political organization as *my* government which is the *slave's* government also" (IV, 360). Washing one's hands clean of evil meant dissolving the connection with government and refusing to obey any legislative acts which were unjust when measured by the higher law. The soldier must refuse to serve in the unjust war, the government official must resign his position, plain people such as Henry Thoreau must refuse to pay their taxes—and all, if necessary, submit to whatever punishment the State might mete out.

Thoreau believed that in advocating and practicing this sort of action he was bringing his enmity to bear directly on the slave power and was freeing himself from that waiting for the majority which he found repugnant in politics. When the Concord sheriff met him and demanded the tax, Thoreau was on his way to the shoemaker. When he was released from jail the next morning (someone having paid his tax in the night), he put on his mended shoe and went off to captain a huckleberry party which had perhaps been planned a few days earlier. He had done his duty and could attend to his private concerns. But he realized himself that as far as the abolition of slavery was concerned the success of his tactic depended on numbers. One man might easily be jailed without serious consequence to the State. But what if he were multiplied by a hundred, by a thousand? Even if the men of principle were numerically still a minority, they would seriously interfere with the operation of the State. "If the alternative is to keep all just men in prison, or give up war and slavery, the State," he concluded, "will not hesitate which to choose." What he was presenting was "the definition of a peaceable revolution, if any such is possible" (IV, 371).

But though he recognized that success depended on numbers, he seems to have made no effort to gain support among the abolitionists of Concord and Boston. The truth was to speak for itself. He conceived of revolutionary action as the spontaneous parallel activity of numerous minds each individually and independently obedient to the higher law. The daily life of a Birney or a Phillips or a Douglass, the endless writing, haranguing, traveling, bargaining, searching for support and money—all this was outside both his genius and his opinions. It is not surprising, then, that the just men and women whose support was to transform the refusal to pay a poll tax from an act of individual protest to an act of revolution did not turn up. He had gone to jail alone, and after his lecture on resistance to government made public the rationale of his action, he remained alone still.

III

As was suggested earlier, this theory of social action was peculiarly suited to Thoreau's temperament, which embraced two poles of quietism and militancy.

In a journal entry written two years after Thoreau's abandonment of the Walden hut, Emerson listed Europe's great representative men, whom he labeled "Big-Endians," next to their American counterparts, the "Little-Endians." Alcott, for example, corresponded to Plato, Emerson himself to Goethe. Opposite Thoreau was Napoleon.[22] A dozen years later, when Thoreau was dead and Emerson could review more impersonally their mixed intimacy and antagonism, he reiterated the belief that Thoreau was not merely "contemplative" but that "with his energy and practical ability he seemed born for great enterprise and for command."[23]

This division of personality in Thoreau was congruent with a division of intellect in certain segments of his New England. And when the inconsistency within came to be discussed in his first book, it appeared in its outward form as the "struggle between the Oriental and Occidental in every nation" (I, 147). The poles he thus names are contemplation and action, stagnancy and progress; their symbols are the Brahman and Christ.

The essential premise of the Brahman as Thoreau pictures him is that a man lives singly in relation to deity and not in society with other men. The social fates will assign him a calling which he must follow, but he is to carry out its tasks without any thought to their consequences and without any wish for reward. All the multitude of desires which spring from the body and from society he is to suppress, for his wisdom is confirmed "when, like the tortoise, he can draw in all his members, and restrain them from their wonted purposes,"[24] and having thus purified his soul, he can reach for the finality of "an immense consolation," an "eternal absorption in Brahma" (I, 141).

Limited by this concept of the goal of life, the Brahman philosophers dwell on all that is static, such as the "inevitability and unchangeableness of laws," the "power of temperament and constitution," and the "circumstances, or birth and affinity." But "buoyancy, freedom, flexibility, variety, possibility, which also," writes Thoreau,

---

[22] Edward W. Emerson and Waldo E. Forbes, eds., *Journals of Ralph Waldo Emerson* (10 vols.; Boston and New York, 1912), VIII, 62.

[23] "Biographical Sketch" of Thoreau, in the latter's *Writings,* I, xxxv.

[24] Quoted by Thoreau, I, 144.

"are qualities of the Unnamed, they deal not with" (I, 141). The consequence of their philosophy for society is a conservatism "as wide as the world, and as unwearied as time, preserving the universe with Asiatic anxiety, in that state in which it appeared to their minds" (I, 140). The consequence for the successful individual is twofold. He attains the "moral grandeur and sublimity" (I, 148) of the bibles of his religion. But as he retracts his humanity until all is within the shell and the shell itself begins to condense toward the pinpoint of spirituality, he gains also a rotting isolation. "Infinitely wise," comments Thoreau, "yet infinitely stagnant" (I, 141).

The same Asia which produced the Brahman also produced his counterpart and opposite, "the prince of Reformers and Radicals." Christ was not content to be simply "a child of God"; he was "a brother of mankind" as well, and instead of being "absorbed into Brahm," sought to bring Brahm "down to earth and to mankind." His philosophy was above all things practical. "There is no harmless dreaming" in the New Testament, writes Thoreau, "no wise speculation in it, but everywhere a substratum of good sense. It never *reflects*, but it *repents*" (I, 141 f.). While the Brahman "has nothing to do in this world," the Christian is "full of activity." He does not tolerate evil hoping to "starve it out," but proceeds "courageously to assault" it. His aim is not to contemplate but to transform (I, 146 f.).

Viewing this contradictory pair chronologically, Thoreau discovered both succession and contemporaneity. The plants of the Orient had symbolically given way to those of the Occident: "already has the era of the temperate zone arrived, the era of the pine and the oak, for the palm and the banian do not supply the wants of this age." But just as Occidental berries and evergreens on the Himalayan slopes overlooked Oriental India, "so did this active modern life have even then a foothold and lurking-place in the midst of the stateliness and contemplativeness of those Eastern plains" (I, 258). And correspondingly, Thoreau and his brother might still lead "a dignified Oriental life" along the cold Merrimack River in 1839, taking "the maple and the alders" for their "Kát-trees," whose drugs disposed the Oriental mind to revery (I, 130). Neither opposite wholly excludes the other: "there is a struggle between the Oriental and Occidental in every nation."

The identical struggle as it existed in his own personality and opinions Thoreau projected in the favorite image of time and eternity. Is there history? he asks. At intervals, all succession seems to telescope into contemporaneity, and the generations of men gather concentrically about the sun of deity, all simultaneously visible to it. Companions in time fade off to left and right, leaving only the single person trying to see God. Change is illusion. There has always been "but the sun and eye," and "the ages have not added a new ray to the one, nor altered a fibre of the other" (I, 164). Farmers in Concord and their seeming ancestors in Egypt, distant in time, are neighbors in eternity, and Thoreau is an Oriental, living singly in relation to deity, indifferent to time and place, "becalmed in the infinite leisure and repose of nature" (I, 130). But in the internodes of these experiences of stasis, time and history and progress are true reality. The world moves forward by practicing what it first rejected as heresy, and the duty of man is to be an innovating master of the art of life. What was new for Egypt has long been old for Concord. Contemporaneity again expands to succession, and if man still looks to deity, he must also regard his own country and generation.

It is not difficult to see the parallel between this employment of the image and that cited earlier. The Orient, the Brahman, and the eternal reflect that Thoreau who was not born to change the world and make the world better but to change himself and make himself better. Time, and Christ, and the Occident are the militant reformer in him and the man devoted to the ends of the body rather than to the ends of the soul. What his theory of social action aimed at was the reconciliation of these opposites.

It was this reconciliation that was Thoreau's problem at Walden and perhaps, it may be suggested, of his entire life. The synthesis attempted at the pond, however, proved unsuccessful. Had he practiced an undiluted perfectionism, he might perhaps have isolated himself from the men and women of whose movements he was a part. But once he attempted—from whatever distance—to bring to bear the lever which would dislodge evil, he brought himself back into the world from which he had withdrawn and became subject to the pressures of reality which affected the social movements of his day. These pressures forced him in a direction opposite to the one on which he had set out. An examination of the three aspects of his experiment relevant to the economy—its relation to Northern capitalism, Southern slavery, and to nature—will document this conflict.

IV

Thoreau's ideal economic unit—the single homestead based on subsistence agriculture and handicrafts—belongs in the context of the movement to settle the frontier. When he condemned his neighbor John Field for hiring himself out as a laborer instead of following Thoreau's own example, it was for "thinking to live by some derivative old-country mode in this primitive new country" (VII, 384). He took for granted the availability of land, going so far as to suggest that his ascetic yeoman might find it easier to "select a fresh spot from time to time than to manure the old" (II, 61), and he assumed an extreme fluidity of social relations not to be found in a more settled economy. That men gave themselves over to coarse labor and pursued false goals "even in this comparatively free country" was owing, he thought, to "mere ignorance and mistake." Their fate in life was only "a seeming fate" and their obedience to it "a blind obedience" (II, 6). They appeared to have "deliberately chosen the common mode of living because they preferred it to any other" (II, 9). Men deluded themselves with the thought that there was no choice left, but it seemed to Thoreau that a correct assessment of their reality would prove otherwise.

When Thoreau took a vacation from Walden Pond in the summer of 1846 and traveled to Maine, he found confirmation of his belief that here was a new land in which a self-reliant man might establish a new way of life. It was a country, he wrote in "Ktaadn," "full of evergreen trees, of mossy silver birches and watery maples, the ground dotted with insipid small, red berries, and strewn with damp and moss-grown rocks,—a country diversified with innumerable lakes and rapid streams, peopled with trout . . . salmon, shad, and pickerel, and other fishes; the forest resounding at rare intervals with the note of the chickadee, the blue jay, and the woodpecker, the scream of the fish hawk and the eagle, the laugh of the loon, and the whistle of ducks along the solitary streams" (III, 89). It was "the home of the moose, the bear, the caribou, the wolf, the beaver, and the Indian" (III, 89).

This environment easily available for exploitation, where fishing, hunting, lumbering, and farming would find a virgin abundance, represented to Thoreau that "blissful, innocent Nature . . . ever in her spring," which is always inviting mankind to her bosom. "What a place to live, what a place to die and be buried in!" he exclaimed (III, 89 f). Here "on the edge of the wilderness, on Indian Millinocket Stream, in a new world, far in the dark of a continent," a man might "live, as it were, in the primitive age of the world, a primitive man," and "have a flute to play at evening here, while his strains echo to the stars, amid the howling of wolves" (III, 87). He was no further in thought from Walden than the day before he left it.

Nor was it Maine or the frontier alone that was open to sturdy men willing to strike out in a new direction. Thoreau was reminded by his journey of "how exceedingly new this country still is." One had "only to travel for a few days into the interior and back parts even of many of the old States" to find the very same America which had greeted the earliest explorers. We had barely discovered the shores. Behind still loomed a continent; and even the coast, seen intimately by the slow traveler on foot, looked less like a "discovered and settled country" than a "desolate island, and No-Man's Land." We had "advanced by leaps to the Pacific" but had "left many a lesser Oregon and California unexplored behind us" (III, 90 f.).

The enterprising farmer would have forests to transform into grain fields, but Thoreau summarized the procedure so concisely as almost to cover the drudgery: "The mode of clearing and planting is to fell the trees, and burn at once what will burn, then cut them up into suitable lengths, roll into heaps, and burn again; then, with a hoe, plant potatoes where you can come at the ground between the stumps and charred logs; for a first crop the ashes sufficing for manure, and no hoeing being necessary the first year. In the fall, cut, roll, and burn again, and so on, till the land is cleared; and soon it is ready for grain, and to be laid down" (III, 15).

Every man might establish a fruitful life for himself on a new basis if only he were willing. "Let those talk of poverty and hard times who will in the towns and cities," wrote Thoreau. The man who was truly determined to live could scrape together the fare from Boston or New York to Maine—Thoreau's was three dollars—"and be as rich as he pleases, where land costs virtually nothing, and houses only the labor of building, and he may begin life as Adam did" (III, 15 f.).

The movement to settle the frontier, in which Thoreau placed himself with the lectures on his experiment at the pond and on his first trip to Maine, was a coalition embracing diverse ideologies and providing a temporary and shifting common ground for such unlike figures as a Horace Greeley and a Lewis Masquerier.

Horace Greeley conceived of agrarianism in the West as an adjunct to his support of industrialism in the East. The opportunity to acquire a parcel of public land cheaply and easily, he said on one occasion, "would improve the condition of the laboring class in our cities, not by drawing away all to the new lands of the West, but by so enlarging the stream of emigration thither as to diminish the pressure of competition in the labor market throughout the country, and enable the hireling to make terms with his employer as to the duration of his daily toil and the amount of his recompense." It would also "enlarge immensely the demand for the products of our manufactories and workshops, and thus aid the laborers remaining in the Old States by increasing the demand for their labor as well as diminishing the competition to supply it."[25]

For Lewis Masquerier, on the contrary, land reform was a method of destroying whatever factories existed and preventing the development of new ones. Underlying his social thought were the premises that "it is impossible to work as a hireling without losing a portion of the profit of labor" and that therefore "labor and homestead and capital must be combined in the same persons, and not all the labor in one class and the capital in another." He would "destroy these overgrowing cities of the earth and leave only ware-houses, foundries, ship-yards, etc., at the great sea and river ports of the earth for the accommodation of international commerce." The people would move out of the cities, acquire homesteads, and organize themselves in largely self-sufficient townships under a constitution which would

---

[25] Horace Greeley, *Hints Toward Reforms* (2d ed.; New York, 1854), p. 317 f.

abolish "every form of hired and chattel slavery." Thus, he wrote, "agricultural and mechanical labor can be combined in the same person or a part of the family may work at one end and part at the other," with the necessary exchange of products organized "according to the time of labor in their production."[26]

Greeley's vision of new markets was closer to the truth than Masquerier's "Paradise of Rural Cities." Whatever may have been the dreams of certain of its participants, the agrarian movement gradually merged with the expansion of the country and helped create an agriculture in the West which was the complement of the industry of the East, so that in time a single economy covered the continent. Masquerier and many another hoped and perhaps believed that in encouraging the settling of unoccupied land they were helping establish a new utopia. But if they helped anything it was the very social structure they disapproved of.

When Henry Thoreau removed to Walden Pond, his mind was on a utopia not unrelated to Lewis Masquerier's, in which a man would neither work for another nor hire another, but live to himself, eating what he grew, growing only what he ate, and avoiding as much as possible all trade and barter. He did not plan to establish this utopia for himself altogether, but chiefly to demonstrate its practicability.

What he did in actuality was to set himself up in an unproductive and bypassed corner of Massachusetts as a marginal commercial farmer whose cash crop did not bring in enough money to satisfy his needs and who therefore hired himself out as a day laborer in order to make ends meet. He learned, he says, that he could easily raise a "bushel or two of rye and Indian corn . . . and grind them in a hand-mill, and so do without rice and pork" and that if he needed a "concentrated sweet" he could make molasses out of pumpkins or beets or perhaps set out a few maple trees (II, 71). But what he actually did was to plant a cash crop to which even he could apparently not limit his diet—beans—and with its proceeds buy the rice and pork, the rye and Indian meal, the sugar and molasses.

---

[26] Lewis Masquerier, *Sociology* (New York, 1877), pp. 64, 70, 13, 88, 13, 14.

Again, when he thought of the ideal life possible in the Maine woods, it was of a man living in the very midst of nature, "in the primitive age of the world" as it were, "a primitive man," that same life reduced to essentials that he had dreamed of for Walden, where a man "could no longer accuse institutions and society, but must front the true source of evil" (III, 18)—that is, come face to face with his inner self. But Thoreau's directions to the frontiersman dealt with the quickest way to establish a commercial farm, the first crops being of potatoes and as soon as possible after these, others of grain to be shipped to market. The men from the back country whom he praises are hardy and determined individualists, one of whom certainly pleased Thoreau by saying that "for his own part, he wanted no neighbors,—he didn't wish to see any road by his house" (III, 27). But there is no hint about them of an ideal economy or a high aim in life.

Whatever utopia Thoreau may have had in mind, he demonstrated at Walden that a poor but determined man could live on the smallest of homesteads if he were close enough to a town where he might earn supplementary income; and he advocated in "Ktaadn" that dissatisfied individuals remove to unoccupied lands on the frontier or in the bypassed regions behind it, where they might establish their independence on easily available unexploited soil.

It is thus not surprising that the chief publicist of both the experiment and "Ktaadn" was none other than Horace Greeley. After Thoreau lectured on his life in the woods to an audience in Portland, Maine, in the early spring of 1849,[27] Greeley's *Tribune* printed a brief description of his economic venture at Walden, concluding, "If all our young men would but hear this lecture, we think some among them would feel less strongly impelled either to come to New-York or go to California."[28] Similarly, Greeley gave almost four columns to extracts from "Ktaadn," including the paragraphs in which Thoreau reminds his readers of the opportunities for settlement on the frontier and on unimproved acres behind it.[29]

Thoreau's favorite walks in later years were in the most rural

---

[27] Walter Harding, "A Check List of Thoreau's Lectures," *Bulletin of the New York Public Library,* LIII (February 1948), 81.

[28] *New-York Weekly Tribune,* April 7, 1849, p. [5].

[29] *New-York Weekly Tribune,* November 25, 1848, p. [4].

acres of Concord township, which lay west and southwest of the Center. He did not know, he wrote in "Walking," "how significant it is, or how far it is an evidence of singularity, that an individual should thus consent in his pettiest walk with the general movement of the race," but felt that there was "something akin to the migratory instinct in birds and quadrupeds" which "affects both nations and individuals, either perennially or from time to time" (V, 218 f.). He seems to have dimly recognized that force which moved him, not in the direction of his conscious ideals, but in the direction being taken by the country.

V

The same force, though with slight momentum, operated in young Thoreau's attitude to slavery. His approach to this problem was essentially that of the loose coalition of abolitionists clustered around Garrison's *Liberator*. A few months after Thoreau's night in Concord jail, Wendell Phillips spoke in defense of Garrisonian policy at Faneuil Hall, in Boston, and laid greatest stress on the self-interest which kept most Americans out of the antislavery ranks and which forced abolitionists to turn for help to the minority of principled men and women who would follow conscience rather than pocket.

Slavery, Phillips maintained, was not the problem of a region but of the entire nation, for the Southern plantation was economically dependent on Northern bankers and merchants. His hearers themselves were "sitting in the very bulwarks of the slave system," and New England's "wharves had not been of granite, her palaces had not been of marble, but that slave and white man both were robbed at the South by the jugglery of Yankee cunning." So firmly was slavery emplaced, he believed, that none of the common modes of social action could dislodge it, least of all politics. The slave power could "say to political parties, as the Quaker said to the Justice of the Peace, who, in full swollen dignity, attempted to overawe William Penn— 'Good man, my friend *makes* such things as thou.'" The only groups upon which abolitionists could rely were those inspired by the "deep, vital idea of *duty*." Nothing was strong enough to do battle with slavery but "the religious element in the nature of man."[30]

---

[30] "Sketch of the Remarks of Wendell Phillips, at the Faneuil Hall Bazaar, December 29, 1846," *Liberator*, XVII (January 8, 1847), 7.

The men and women whose abolitionism was dictated by their conception of religious duty found other injunctions in the higher law as well and insisted, to one degree or another, that their antislavery crusade be conducted only in ways consistent with these principles. The perfectionists would participate in the abolitionist movement only so long as it did not interfere with the search for sinlessness, the no-organizationists would replace organized associated action by spontaneous parallel individual actions, and the nonresistants would not approve of force or voting or any participation in politics. The internal history of the wing of antislavery led by Phillips and Garrison is the record of the conflict between these a priori, absolute injunctions and the necessities of the practical problem of ending slavery. From time to time, and especially at such critical moments as the founding of the Liberty Party, the passage of the Fugitive Slave Law, the raid on Harper's Ferry, and the outbreak of the Civil War, certain members of the coalition had to choose between discarding their principles or separating from the movement. So ingrained were these beliefs, so integral a part of the ethos of these largely self-made and invariably stubborn thinkers, that their abandonment proved extraordinarily difficult and in some instances impossible.

Among those least responsive to the pressure of the times was Henry Thoreau, who never voted and who abandoned his early no-organization views only to the extent of approving such a unit as John Brown's military platoon—and that for others rather than for himself. But an examination of Thoreau's position on antislavery in the forties discerns two distinct forces, one leading him away from the movement and toward perfectionism, the other toward the direct assault on slavery which he was later to approve in Brown.

There were at least a few among Thoreau's contemporaries who held that the only acceptable strategy for the elimination of slavery lay in the perfection of the individual. Chief among these was John Humphrey Noyes.

Until he became a perfectionist, Noyes considered himself a follower of William Lloyd Garrison, whose tactics at that time included both propaganda and politics. He had been among the few to support Garrison when the latter launched the *Liberator* in 1831, and in

1833 he had helped found the New Haven Anti-Slavery Society. In the winter of 1836–37, following the religious experience which led him to perfectionism, Noyes published a personal Declaration of Independence in which he severed connections with the government of the United States and declared himself one of "the Lord's freemen, . . . free citizens of the world and subjects of the federal government of Jesus Christ," maintaining that Christ's government had superseded all others. Having thus dissociated himself from what he considered evil, he set about destroying it (as he thought) by raising aloft the banner of individual purification.

To Garrison and all other abolitionists he wrote that they would "set Anti-Slavery in the sunshine only by making it tributary to holiness" and that they would "most assuredly throw it into the shade" if they allowed it to occupy that first place "which ought to be occupied by universal emancipation from sin." "I counsel you," he exhorted, "if you love the post of honor—the fore-front of the hottest battle of righteousness—to set your face toward perfect holiness."[31]

Among Noyes's original associates were certain men and women long ago forgotten—James Boyle, for instance, his wife Laura, and T. R. Gates—who refused to join Noyes in the perfectionist community at Oneida and supported instead a combined perfectionism and individualism. Perfectionists, Boyle is said to have declared, "will not be taught of each other, as they are all taught of God, nor will they acknowledge any man as a leader or chief or any thing of the kind."[32]

The parallel between the thesis of the perfectionists, particularly the individualists among them, and the view expressed by Thoreau in *The Service* is apparent and need not be labored. But the year after Thoreau completed that essay, he demonstrated that he was of two minds on the subject of how to handle slavery.

Early in 1841, the thinkers in his home town participated in the discussion of the merits of resistance and nonresistance which had

---

[31] John Humphrey Noyes, "Perfectionism Not Pro-Slavery," *Perfectionist,* III (October 1, 1843), 61.

[32] Quoted in William A. Hinds, *American Communities and Co-Operative Colonies* (Chicago, 1908), p. 167.

been going on for several years among the New England abolitionists. During the first week in February, Adin Ballou arrived, as Emerson wrote, "to christianize us children of darkness in Concord with his Non Resistance."[33] Ballou was the leading figure among the New England pacifists, a man who held that nothing would destroy slavery except "the power of that holiness which grows out of love supreme to our Creator and love unalloyed to our neighbor,"[34] and it was perhaps of his view that Thoreau wrote: "The love which is preached nowadays is an ocean of new milk for a man to swim in. I hear no surf nor surge, but the winds coo over it" (VII, 287 n.). Ten days earlier there had been a debate in the town lyceum on the question "Is it ever proper to offer forcible resistance?" and it was as though to counter its effects that Ballou arrived in town. The side of non-resistance in that debate had been taken by Bronson Alcott, the side of violence by the Thoreau brothers, John and Henry.[35]

It was between the perfectionism of his Brahman and the direct assault of his Christ that Thoreau made compromises while at Walden and for the rest of his short life, with the drift of the nation gradually modifying the proportions in favor of the direct assault.

The compromise which Thoreau attempted while at the pond was rejected by his contemporaries. He did indeed have the sympathy of Alcott, who had himself led the way in refusing to pay taxes, and who defended Thoreau's act against the criticism of Emerson.[36] But the Garrisonian abolitionists, among whom alone he could expect support, had already decided that the tactic was not for them.

Thoreau regarded his individual dissolution of the union between himself and Massachusetts as an application of the Garrisonian policy of "No Union With Slaveholders" (IV, 366). This policy sprang partly from the refusal of perfectionists and nonresistants to recognize

---

[33] Ralph L. Rusk, ed., *The Letters of Ralph Waldo Emerson* (6 vols.; New York, 1939), II, 379.

[34] Adin Ballou, *A Discourse on the Subject of Slavery, Delivered . . . in Mendon, Mass., July 4, 1837* (Boston, 1837), p. 7.

[35] Harding, "A Check List of Thoreau's Lectures," p. 79.

[36] Odell Shepard, ed., *The Journals of Bronson Alcott* (Boston, 1938), p. 183 f.

human government and partly from a belief that the nation-wide strength of slavery made it impossible for a political party to be un-compromisingly abolitionist. It condemned the Federal Constitution as a pro-slavery document and proclaimed that "secession from the present United States Government is the duty of every abolitionist."[37] By secession the Garrisonians meant that until such time as a govern-ment was established which they considered just, individual men and women should resign public office and refuse to vote, and individual states should secede from the Union. Their hope was that slavery in the South would fail if isolated from its sources of trade and money in the North. But they did not suggest that their adherents should stop paying taxes.

The nonresistants among them did not believe in disobeying the law. In 1840, Garrison had denied his aid to one Charles Stearns in his refusal to pay a fine for not training with the militia, arguing that since fines, like taxes, were a tribute exacted by the government, their payment was not necessarily an expression of approval.[38] Four years later, replying to those political abolitionists who objected that paying taxes was at least as criminal support of the union with slavery as voting, Garrison maintained the identical position, writing that the man who had seceded from the Union would "consent peaceably to yield up what is demanded of him" much as he would "give up his purse to a highwayman."[39] The same argument was also put forward by Wendell Phillips, who had never been either a perfectionist or a nonresistant and had adopted the "No Union" policy not as the dictate of a higher law but as what he took for practical politics.[40]

Thoreau, like the Garrisonians, continued to believe in the dissolu-tion of the Union all through the fifties. But when he mentioned this strategy in "Slavery in Massachusetts" in 1854, he said nothing about

---

[37] Quoted in [Wendell P. and Francis J. Garrison], *William Lloyd Garrison, 1805–1879; the Story of His Life Told by His Children* (4 vols.; New York, 1885–89), III, 99.

[38] *Ibid.*, II, 390 f. (footnote).

[39] Quoted in *ibid.*, III, 106.

[40] George L. Austin, *The Life and Times of Wendell Phillips* (Boston, 1884), p. 118 f.

the specific tactic of withholding one's taxes (IV, 403). And in the tax book of the town of Concord for 1849—the year of the publication of "Civil Disobedience"—the notation opposite his name is "Paid."[41] What he had described in that essay was his position "at present," and he had added that a man must see "that he does only what belongs to himself and to the hour" (IV, 381).

VI

Thoreau quotes in one of his early journals a French author's distinction between two views of science: Plato's, which "gives science sublime counsels" and "directs her toward the regions of the ideal," and Aristotle's, which "gives her positive and severe laws, and directs her toward a practical end" (VII, 440). The distinction corresponds to the division between wish and reality in young Thoreau's relation to nature.

Associated with the contemplative pole of his temperament was a yearning for mystical penetration to the ideal behind the visible. "If we see the reality in things," he writes in *A Week*, "of what moment is the superficial and apparent longer? What are the earth and all its interests beside the deep surmise which pierces and scatters them? While I sit here listening to the waves which ripple and break on this shore, I am absolved from all obligation to the past, and the council of nations may reconsider its votes. The grating of a pebble annuls them" (I, 383). Elsewhere in the same book he declares that the "most glorious fact" in his experience is not anything he has done or may hope to do "but a transient thought, or vision, or dream" which he has had; he would give "all the wealth of the world, and all the deeds of all the heroes, for one true vision" (I, 145 f.).

The connection between this quietism and the experiment at Walden was glimpsed by Harrison Blake, one of the few whom we may call Thoreau's friends. Shortly after Thoreau had left the pond to enter Emerson's household, Blake, moved by forces in his own

---

[41] Viola C. White, "Check List of Thoreau Items in the Abernethy Library of Middlebury College," in Reginald L. Cook, *The Concord Saunterer* (Middlebury, Vermont, 1940), p. 77.

development, reread Thoreau's early essay on Persius and was led to write him a letter describing "a haunting impression" of their first meeting. "When I was last in Concord," he wrote, "you spoke of retiring farther from civilization. I asked you if you would feel no longings for the society of your friends. Your reply was in substance, 'No, I am nothing.'" Moved by the "depth of resources" and the "completeness of renunciation" in this answer, Blake was able to find a "new significance" in the idea that "God is here, that we have but to bow before Him in profound submission at every moment, and He will fill our souls with his presence." "I honor you," he wrote gratefully to Thoreau, "because you abstain from action, and open your soul that you may *be* somewhat" (VI, 158 f.).

Over and over again in the pages of his earlier writings, Thoreau can be seen opening his soul to the influx of spirit. At rare moments —such as that at the pond when he sat in his "sunny doorway from sunrise till noon, rapt in a revery, amidst the pines and hickories and sumachs, in undisturbed solitude and stillness"—he so abstracted himself that he rested in eternity until the sun sinking to his window or "the noise of some traveller's wagon on the distant highway" re-called him to "the lapse of time" (II, 123 f.). More often, as in the justly celebrated passage in *Walden* dividing the foundations of his ideal life from its riches, he was seeking and hoping: "Time is but the stream I go a-fishing in. I drink at it; but while I drink I see the sandy bottom and detect how shallow it is. Its thin current slides away, but eternity remains. I would drink deeper; fish in the sky, whose bottom is pebbly with stars" (II, 109).

Distinct from this approach to nature was that which looked for rigorous laws and practical applications. Early in 1846, Thoreau surveyed Walden Pond, sounded its bottom, and embodied his results in a map which later adorned the title page of his famous book. His motives, as he explains them, were to locate the inlet or outlet of the pond and to convince his townsmen of the uniformity of nature. There were some in Concord who believed that Walden was a Bot-tomless Pond and others who feared that its pure water concealed dangerous chasms. Thoreau discovered no inlet or outlet save "rain and snow and evaporation" but thought such places might be found with thermometer and line, since "where the water flows into the

pond it will probably be coldest in summer and warmest in winter"
(II, 322). Neither did he discover unexpected depths, measurable or
otherwise. Man's imagination, he concluded, given "the least license,
dives deeper and soars higher than Nature goes" (II, 318).

His most interesting discoveries, those which led onward to laws
and practice, involved the interrelations among the recorded observations. Even while he was still taking soundings, he noticed what
seemed a roughly predictable relationship between the bottom of the
pond and the contours of the surrounding countryside. "The regu-
larity of the bottom and its conformity to the shores and the range of
the neighboring hills were so perfect that a distant promontory betrayed itself in the soundings quite across the pond, and its direction
could be determined by observing the opposite shore." Cape became
bar, "plain shoal, and valley and gorge deep water and channel" (II,
318). Later, when he examined the map, he also discovered a "remarkable coincidence": that the pond was deepest at the very point
which marked the intersection of the lines of its greatest length and
greatest breadth (II, 319).

What he thought of this coincidence of horizontal and vertical
maxima at that time we cannot tell, for the original journals of the
period are unavailable. But by the spring of 1852, if not sooner, he
had begun to think that more might be involved than simple chance.
In March of that year, having surveyed it earlier (VIII, 164), he
sounded White Pond (IX, 345), another of the numerous small lakes
of his native township, to see how nearly he could guess at its deepest
point "by observing the outlines of its surface and the character of its
shores alone" (II, 320). Since "the line of greatest breadth fell very
near the line of least breadth, where two opposite capes approached
each other and two opposite bays receded," he "ventured to mark a
point a short distance from the latter line, but still on the line of greatest depth, as the deepest" (II, 320). Soundings found the deepest
point within a hundred feet of his mark and still farther in the same
direction in which he had inclined.

It was a characteristic of transcendentalism, and especially of
young Thoreau's variety, that it attempted to close the gap between
the nature usually sought through mysticism and the nature usually
studied by science. The doctrine of correspondence, which held that

the physical and biological facts of nature were symbols of the spiritual and moral facts of deity, was an expression of the essential unity of the transcendentalist cosmos. All was oversoul in varying forms. All moved in accordance with identical laws, expressed in parallel in the moral and physical orders. Hence, argued Thoreau in *A Week*, the laws of science and of morality interpenetrated one another, and ultimately "we might so simplify the rules of moral philosophy, as well as of arithmetic, that one formula would express them both" (I, 386). A law of science, raised to the proper level of abstraction, would encompass its parallel in morality and attain a new beauty and universality.

The view of nature as mere symbol did not, however, wholly satisfy Thoreau, who wished, in the very glimpsing of the spiritual, to retain firm hold on the material. He seems to have owned an instinctive materialism so tenacious that it would not surrender to transcendentalist idealism but combined with it instead to become the dominant partner in an earthy pantheism.

Thoreau's own presentation of the collision of these two views is preserved in one of his college themes. The subject assigned was the sort of mind that refuses to accept popular opinion, and Thoreau chose to describe the liberation of a thinking man from that prejudice of the mass which holds the senses to be "the supreme arbiters, from whose decision there is no appeal." On the day of new insight, the clarity of the commonplace heaven is overshadowed by clouds of mystery expanding, multiplying, rising on all sides from the horizon to the zenith, and the thinker experiences his crisis: "The earth was once firm beneath the feet, but it now affords but a frail support,— its solid surface is as yielding and elastic as air. The grass grew and water ran, and who so blind as to question their reality. A feeling of loneliness comes over the soul, for these things are of the past." After the storms without and within have subsided, the "embryo philosopher" announces his new opinion, accepting only spirit in its various forms, and then betrays himself in the conclusion: "all things else which his obstinate and self-willed senses present to him, are plainly, though unaccountably, absurd."[42]

---

[42] Edwin I. Moser, ed., "Henry David Thoreau: the College Essays" (unpublished master's thesis, New York University, 1951), pp. 145–49.

Thoreau's "obstinate and self-willed senses" continued to transmit an external world which it seemed to him was not mere projection of spirit but existed in its own right. Like Dr. Johnson kicking the stone, Thoreau wrote in *A Week*, "the landscape is indeed something real, and solid, and sincere, and I have not put my foot through it yet" (I, 374). It comforted him to believe that the material world had an existence he could rely on. That tract on the bank of the Concord called Conantum—"the old deserted farmhouse, the desolate pasture with its bleak cliff, the open wood, the river-reach, the green meadow in the midst, and the moss-grown wild-apple orchard"—was not merely a vision he could remember but a place he could "bodily revisit, and find it even so" (I, 374). But within this outward nature there is commonly for young Thoreau an "ideal or real Nature, infinitely more perfect than the actual."[43] Striving to communicate the interpenetration of these two worlds in visual images, he speaks of concentricity, inner and outer, folds within folds (I, 408 f.). "The world," he writes, "has many rings, like Saturn, and we live now on the outermost of them all" (I, 411).

It followed for him that those "divine germs called the senses" could be educated to a higher purpose, the ear and the eye, now put to "trivial" and "grovelling" uses, taught to "hear celestial sounds" and to "behold beauty now invisible." "May we not *see* God?" he demands. "Are we to be put off and amused in this life, as it were with a mere allegory? Is not Nature, rightly read, that of which she is commonly taken to be the symbol merely?" (I, 408)

It was Thoreau's destiny at the pond to lose hold of his unified world and to move toward empirical research practiced only on its outermost ring. This research, moreover, had practical applications which served the commercial and industrial community in opposition to which he had placed himself.

Working from the assumed correspondence between the physical and the moral, Thoreau saw two parallel possibilities in his discovery about the dimensions of the ponds. What he called the ethical concerned the reflections of a man's inner personality in his outward

---

[43] From Thoreau's journal entry for November 2, 1843, quoted in F. B. Sanborn, *The First and Last Journeys of Thoreau* (Boston, 1905), I, 85.

actions and was no more than the opinion common among the transcendentalists that each man make his own fate. Lines drawn "through the length and breadth of the aggregate of a man's particular daily behaviors and waves of life into his coves and inlets" should intersect to reveal "the height or depth of his character." Similarly, we might discover the inner man by knowing "how his shores trend" and what are his "adjacent country or circumstances." For "if he is surrounded by mountainous circumstances, an Achillean shore, whose peaks overshadow and are reflected in his bosom, they suggest a corresponding depth in him. But a low and smooth shore proves him shallow on that side" (II, 321). It was a noble conception, that certain radical laws underlie both nature and society, but incapable of any but the most mechanical reading into nature of the ideas of a particular body of men.

Thoreau's second possibility concerned the expression of the totality of a complex situation of physical nature in a single one of its component elements. "If we knew all the laws of Nature," he wrote, describing the ideal limit of this process, "we should need only one fact, or the description of one actual phenomenon, to infer all the particular results at that point" (II, 320). Thus a knowledge of the greatest length and breadth of a pond equips us to predict the point of greatest depth, and a knowledge of the shores and surrounding terrain provides information about the contour of the bottom.

Perhaps, he speculated, the surface dimensions of a harbor might be in a predictable relation to the depth of its water. He had noticed that three of the five coves of Walden Pond had bars across their mouths and that "in proportion as the mouth of the cove was wider compared with its length, the water over the bar was deeper compared with that in the basin. Given then the length and breadth of the cove, and the character of the surrounding shore," he concluded, "and you have almost elements enough to make out a formula for all cases." Such a formula would also apply to comparable formations, including harbors, for "every harbor on the sea-coast, also, has its bar at its entrance" (II, 319). Only a short distance separated the subsistence experiment at Walden from Boston with its docks and warehouses.

During the years in which Thoreau pursued his isolated trade with the "Celestial Empire" at Walden, the United States Coast Survey was continually busy with its study of our seacoast and of the harbors of Boston, New York, and other centers, not a small part of whose activities also involved trade with a Celestial Empire. How much Thoreau knew of the activities of the Survey while he was at the pond we cannot tell. When he writes that by sounding through the ice he could "determine the shape of the bottom with greater accuracy than is possible in surveying harbors which do not freeze over" (II, 318), he is obviously referring to the work of this organization, but the exact date of this passage cannot now be determined. By 1851, at least, he is well acquainted with the Survey, is reading a work on tides and ocean currents by Lieutenant Charles H. Davis,[44] and has discussed the variations of the compass with William Cranch Bond,[45] two of the Survey's leading investigators. When he speculates on a possible law governing the inlets of both ponds and oceans, he is well aware of the direction in which his work is leading him.

The careful technicians who began the systematic investigation of our seacoast did not have their eyes set on laws expressing the unity of the spiritual and physical orders. Fascinated as they undoubtedly were by the significance of their findings for what is sometimes called "pure" knowledge, they were not blind to the immediate and ultimate

---

[44] In a journal entry of July or August, 1850, Thoreau writes that "according to Lieutenant Davis, the forms, extent, and distribution of sandbars and banks are principally determined by tides, not by winds and waves" (VIII, 45; also in *Cape Cod*, IV, 155). Charles Henry Davis, a naval officer who from 1842 to 1849 had conducted research on tides, currents, and related phenomena for the United States Coast Survey (see Charles H. Davis, *Life of Charles Henry Davis, Rear Admiral, 1807-1877* [Boston and New York, 1899], p. 80), published the theory referred to by Thoreau in "A Memoir of the Geological Action of the Tides and Other Currents of the Ocean," communicated to the American Academy of Arts and Sciences on November 8, 1848, and printed in its *Memoirs,* New Series, IV, Part I (1849), 117-56.

[45] Thoreau records a visit to the Harvard Observatory and a conversation with Bond in the journal for July 9, 1851 (VIII, 294). He also reports, in the journal for June 2, 1851, that he has spoken with "John Downes, who is connected with the Coast Survey" (VIII, 224).

cash value of accurate maps and of an understanding of the conflict between sea and shore. In an article defending the Coast Survey against a critic, Lieutenant Davis maintained that its operations were not only approved by learned societies and leading men of science but that statements of "the principal merchants and underwriters in the northern capitals" showed that the Survey "has heretofore rendered, and continues to give, to commerce the most important facilities and improvements."[46] On this point he differed in no way from his opponent, who took exception only to the way in which the organization handled its funds and to the rate at which its work advanced. When *Hunt's Merchants' Magazine* published the article to which Lieutenant Davis was replying, it defended itself against the charge of having left its proper field by stating that the "purposes and results" of the Survey's work "are decidedly commercial, and are fairly connected with the interests of the portion of the community who are our patrons."[47] It was in the direction of service to this portion of the communty that Thoreau's investigations of the pond were necessarily leading him, and it was the same general direction, as we shall see, that he was to follow in his studies of forestry.

As if to complete the dissociation of the integrated ideology which had led him to the pond, Thoreau had what can only be described as the negation of a mystical experience, during which his essential pantheism suddenly dissolved into its component idealism and materialism and shocked him into fear and bewilderment.

When Thoreau climbed Mt. Katahdin on his excursion to Maine, he drew farther and farther away, as he ascended, from that lower region whose virgin plenty had so delighted him. Leaving his companions making camp one sunset, he pulled himself up the sides of a narrow ravine, scrambled on all fours over a dense belt of dwarfed

---

[46] Charles Henry Davis, " 'The Coast Survey of the United States': A Reply to an Article with the Above Title, in the February Number of the Merchants' Magazine," *Hunt's Merchants' Magazine,* XX (April 1849), 402 f.

[47] "Survey of the Coast of the United States," *Hunt's Merchants' Magazine,* XX (February 1849), 132.

black spruce whose branches were the unfinished roofs of bear dens, with the bears "even then at home," and came at length to a height beyond vegetation, "where rocks, gray, silent rocks, were the flocks and herds that pastured," and looked at him "with hard gray eyes." He was reminded of the arduous journey of Milton's Satan through Chaos.

Climbing again the next morning, he was separated from his companions and made his way alone to the summit. The mountain seemed to him "a vast aggregation of loose rocks, as if some time it had rained rocks, and they lay as they fell on the mountain sides, nowhere fairly at rest, but leaning on each other." He was amid the "raw materials" of the planet, in Chaos again, upon "an undone extremity of the globe" where nature does not welcome man but drives him relentlessly before her with monumental desolation. Here a man is "more lone than you can imagine." Some part of him, "even some vital part, seems to escape through the loose grating of his ribs as he ascends. . . . Vast, Titanic, inhuman Nature has got him at a disadvantage, caught him alone, and pilfers him of some of his divine faculty."

What it was that he had lost Thoreau did not learn till later that same day, when he descended the mountain and crossed a strip of burned land over which a new growth of low poplars and blueberries was beginning to spread. It seemed like familiar Concord landscape to him, perhaps "some pasture run to waste, or partially reclaimed by man," but when he asked himself "what man, what brother or sister or kinsman of our race made it and claimed it," he broke out of the circle of ownership and exploitation which was the normal circumference of his relation to nature and saw fully for the first time another nature, "primeval, untamed, forever untamable," "vast and drear and inhuman," "savage and awful, though beautiful."

He looked with awe "to see what the Powers had made there, the form and fashion and material of their work," and found only "Matter, vast, terrific." The effect of this discovery is best communicated in his own words: "What is it to be admitted to a museum, to see a myriad of particular things, compared with being shown some star's surface, some hard matter in its home! I stand in awe of my body, this matter to which I am bound has become so strange to me.

I fear not spirits, ghosts, of which I am one,—*that* my body might,—
but I fear bodies, I tremble to meet them. What is this Titan that has
possession of me? Talk of mysteries! Think of our life in nature,—
daily to be shown matter, to come in contact with it,—rocks, trees,
wind on our cheeks! the *solid* earth! the *actual* world! the *common
sense! Contact! Contact! Who* are we? *where* are we?" (III, 67–79)

The universe pantheistically informed with a benign godhead had
suddenly dissociated into its parts. For the rest of his life he was to
strive in vain to reunite them.

2

Morning Surveyor
and Afternoon Seeker

Thwarted in practice, the utopian impulse turned inward to seek an outlet in imagination. In the closing pages of *Walden* it reappeared divested of the externalities which had clothed it in the opening chapter and in "Ktaadn," preaching neither settlement beyond the frontier nor retreat to bypassed acres, but the seeker's interior walk along "that farthest western way" which is "a tangent to this sphere" (II, 354 f.).

What this expedition to the continent within the self was to uncover was the same inner law which Thoreau had thought he was giving expression to at the pond. There was to be a new grappling for solid bottom lest he again spring an arch before he had got a true foundation. No end was served by building upon an approximation of the absolute which would before long be found to fall short of its referent. "Shall we with pains erect a heaven of blue glass over ourselves," he inquired, "though when it is done we shall be sure to gaze still at the true ethereal heaven far above, as if the former were not?" (II, 359). Better to keep surveying for the true bearings, and if the end of life has not yet witnessed success, at least to preserve the inward youthfulness of the aspirant.

To such exploration of the soul no particular external reality is prerequisite, and Thoreau, no longer projecting new schemes of personal economics for the salvation of his impoverished or dissatisfied neighbors, advised instead: "however mean your life is, meet it and live it" (II, 361). For while it was presumably true, to reverse his sentence, that the ideal represented by the sun was reflected as brightly from the rich man's window as from the windows of the almshouse (II, 361), Thoreau recognized the incompatibility between the internal, creative search which he was advocating and the external, acquisitive one then (and now) socially acceptable, and he addressed himself to the poor, expecting poverty to be the unavoidable partner of idealism. The man who successfully prosecuted the inward voyage would learn to live within acquisitive society and yet above it, liberated from imprisonment within its values. His inevitable lack of means, the isolation of his introspective exploration, his ineffectiveness in the face of organized society—these would lose the qualities they had for the conforming individual, whom they confronted as dangers to be shunned at all costs, and become the matrix of a new life whose essential pattern was a polarity: resignation to the hard lot assigned the opponent of acquisitiveness, and unceasing extrasocietal search for a new absolute on which to found a just life.

Between the poles of this pattern, and unpredictable from either extreme or from their combination, emerged a new motion which led Henry Thoreau away from utopian social thought and toward a new synthesis. But the pattern itself dominated his life for several years after he left the pond—long enough, perhaps, to reach his serious illness of the spring of 1855, which brought his moonlight walks to an end—and remained even to the last as a subordinate framework enclosing an evolution away from its own main elements.

I

To accept life within even though above the prevailing economic order transformed the question of a livelihood from one of principle to one of expediency. No longer a matter of finding an occupation in keeping with the dictates of oversoul, it reduced to a commonplace of that day and ours: the problem of the dedicated individual whose calling has only slight value in the market.

Thoreau had already been forced to test a few solutions to this problem in the school-teaching, pencil-making, odd-jobbing days of the early forties when as "reporter to a journal of no very wide circulation" (the *Dial*, that is) he got only his labor for his pains (II, 19) and when he undertook the sally into Manhattan which failed to convince its editors of his cash value. Now that he had retreated from the pondside to room and board at Emerson's, the question was only prospectively critical pending the return of his patron from a lecture tour in Europe,[1] but it was being increasingly dramatized by experiences with publishers and lyceum secretaries.

By the fall of 1847, a year and more had passed since the manuscript of *A Week* began its round of the publishing houses, meeting rejection in Boston, New York, and Philadelphia.[2] So shaken was Thoreau's self-confidence then that he declared himself "indifferent" (VI, 139) to the fate of this work whose creation had taken the best energies of six years. Eventually, however, he resigned himself to the fact that the same labor and self-denial which had bought time for the book's composition would now have to provide for its publication as well. The full details of the financial arrangement between Thoreau and his publisher Munroe have not yet come to light, but the cost of the edition was probably not very much less than the $450 which Ticknor & Co. belatedly estimated for one thousand copies, half to remain unbound.[3] It was thus not long after leaving Emerson's house that Thoreau found himself in need of an occupation that

---

[1] In *Walden* Thoreau gives September 6, 1847, as the day he left the pond (II, 351). A manuscript page in the Huntington Library gives July 30, 1848, as the day on which he returned to his father's house (HM 13182, cited by permission of the Huntington Library).

[2] A full account of the publication history of Thoreau's first book will be found in James P. Wood, "Mr. Thoreau Writes a Book," *New Colophon*, I (October 1948), 367–76, and in Raymond Adams, "The Bibliographical History of Thoreau's *A Week on the Concord and Merrimack Rivers*," *Papers of the Bibliographical Society of America*, XLIII (First Quarter, 1949), 39–47.

[3] Walter Harding, "The Correspondence of Henry David Thoreau, 1836–1849," unpublished dissertation, Rutgers University, 1950, p. 473 f. Henry S. Canby, in his *Thoreau* (Boston and New York, 1939), p. 278, estimates the cost of the book to Thoreau at $390.

would not merely supply necessities but yield a surplus with which to pay off debts.

Lecturing would very obviously not do. Between the beginning of 1844 (when he came back from New York) and the fall of 1849 (when his thoughts began to turn to surveying), Thoreau delivered only fourteen lectures. At least five of these, and perhaps as many as nine, were before the lyceum in Concord and presumably unpaid for. Of the five remaining, one in Portland netted $20, two in Salem $40.[4] Even had all fourteen paid him at this rate, the resulting sum would not have covered the printing of *A Week*, to say nothing of "Food, Shelter, Clothing, and Fuel." Neither then nor since have American audiences been ready to welcome a radical in politics and ethics who does not hesitate to tell them plainly that he condemns their aims in life and their political parties and that he thinks very little indeed of their religion and its ministers.[5]

Nor were the editors of magazines any more receptive or remunerative than the curators of lyceums. Between the conclusion of the *Dial* and the beginning of his career as a surveyor, Thoreau published a letter in the *Liberator* on the struggle for free speech in the Concord Lyceum, an essay in *Graham's Magazine* on Carlyle, a series of articles in the *Union Magazine* about his first trip to Maine, and the lecture in *Aesthetic Papers* which became known as "Civil Disobedience." The letter on Wendell Phillips and the Concord Lyceum was a communication to the editor and could not have been paid for. For the essay on Carlyle, Thoreau received $50 through Horace Greeley (who had acted as literary agent and taken a fee of $25), waiting for the payment a full year after publication (VI, 169 f.). For the series on Maine, Greeley paid Thoreau $25 and added another $25 after selling it and deducting an equal sum for his own fee and expenses.[6]

---

[4] Walter Harding, "A Check List of Thoreau's Lectures," *Bulletin of the New York Public Library*, LIII (February 1949), 79–82.

[5] For a documentation of the thesis that until the Civil War the lyceums were not open to the expression of reform ideas, see Vern Wagner, "The Lecture Lyceum and the Problem of Controversy," *Journal of the History of Ideas*, XV (January 1954), 119–35.

[6] F. B. Sanborn, *Henry D. Thoreau* (Boston and New York, 1882), p. 226 f.

There is no information on what Thoreau may have received for his most famous essay, but the failure of Elizabeth Peabody's journal after its first number suggests a sum smaller than that which the experienced Greeley could extract from more successful editors— perhaps even nothing.

It was in a letter to Greeley acknowledging the receipt of one of these rare payments that Thoreau, still in Emerson's house in the spring of 1848, announced his intended return to odd-jobbing.[7] The appearance of his Carlyle article in *Graham's Magazine* when he had not yet been paid for it had led him to enlist Greeley's aid in dealing with its editor (VI, 169), and now, applying pride to his hurts, he boasted of his independence of Grahams and Greeleys by describing his success in supporting himself by manual labor. How far Thoreau exaggerated when he claimed that for five years he had had no income save from "the coarsest work of all kinds"[8] and that he had had to work hardly more than a month each in spring and fall to cover his rationed expenses is unimportant beside the pain which must have accompanied this final decision to meet and live his own mean reality. It was not in his character to express pain openly. Earlier that same month he had written to Blake that he supposed he knew "comparatively little" of "acute sorrow," its place being "supplied, perchance, by a certain hard and proportionately barren indifference" (VI, 168). We shall never know how often he may have bitten his lips before leaving the privacy of the Emersons' upstairs chamber in order to satisfy Concord of his stoicism.

When he left his patron's house in midsummer of 1848, Thoreau turned immediately to the manual labor which he had boasted of to Greeley. Emerson's list of his odd jobs probably gives as accurate a picture as is needed: "building a boat or a fence, planting, grafting,

---

[7] Walter Harding provides an accurate text of Thoreau's letter of May 19, 1848, in "Franklin B. Sanborn and Thoreau's Letters," *Boston Public Library Quarterly,* III (October 1951), 288–93. Greeley turned Thoreau's letter to his own account, incorporating its first paragraph (with the exception of the sentence acknowledging receipt of the money) in an editorial headed "A Lesson for Young Poets," which appeared in the *New-York Weekly Tribune,* June 3, 1848, p. 6.

[8] Harding, "Franklin B. Sanborn and Thoreau's Letters," p. 289.

surveying," with "short work" preferred to "long engagements."[9] It corresponds reasonably well with a manuscript record among Thoreau's own papers that covers the second half of 1848 and adds chiefly wallpapering and whitewashing and working in the family pencil shop.[10] It was from these odd jobs that Thoreau drifted (the word is Emerson's[11]) into the trade of surveyor.

The necessities of the Concord economy had not yet precipitated surveying as a distinct full-time trade, and as a Jack-of-all-trades, Thoreau had apparently known how to survey from his youth. At least, a pupil of his at the Concord Academy recalled many years later that Henry and his brother John had taken their boys on a surveying field trip along the river to show them a practical side to the schoolroom's mathematics.[12] Emerson's account book records a payment of one dollar to Thoreau on April 27, 1847, for surveying a newly acquired lot,[13] and before that date Thoreau had completed surveys of at least two Concord landmarks, apparently for his own pleasure. The first, whose plan is dated September 5, 1845, was of the Old Marlborough Road;[14] the second was the survey of Walden Pond carried out in the winter of 1846 and already discussed in these pages. It was not unjustly, therefore, that Thoreau included "surveyor" in the half bitter, half boastful account of his occupations sent to his Harvard classmates in the fall of 1847.[15]

---

[9] "Biographical Sketch," in Thoreau's *Writings,* I, xiv.

[10] Now in the Huntington Library (HM 13182), by whose permission it is here referred to.

[11] "Biographical Sketch," p. xv.

[12] George Keyes, quoted by Edward Waldo Emerson in his notes of an interview that took place about 1890; ms. in the possession of Mr. Raymond Emerson, by whose kind permission it is here mentioned.

[13] Prof. Ralph L. Rusk, who refers to this survey in his biography of Emerson (p. 325), has very kindly informed me of this payment. A plan of "RWE's woodlot by Walden Pond paced with a Pocket Compass at the time he bought it" is in the Concord Free Public Library.

[14] This plan is now in the possession of Mr. John L. Cooley, to whom I am indebted for its description. The date is not in Thoreau's hand, and may be erroneous, and part of the name of the road is missing.

[15] Canby, *Thoreau,* p. 301.

The first survey recorded by Thoreau in the "Field Notes" which preserve the history of his work is that of Isaac Watts' wood lot, made in November 1849 with the compass and chain of the older Concord surveyor Cyrus Hubbard.[16] Thoreau did not acquire a compass of his own till the following year, using it for the first time when he surveyed Jesse Hosmer's farm, a job vaguely dated "Spring, 1850,"[17] but probably not much before the undetermined day in March when he confided to himself that his survey of Emerson's wood lot and meadow had been done "with unusual accuracy."[18] It was perhaps the same spring that a handbill appeared in Concord and neighboring towns advertising Henry D. Thoreau as the man to apply to for surveying "of all kinds, according to the best methods known."[19]

II

No other occupation for which Thoreau qualified would have been as adequately symbolic as was surveying of the decision to accept life within an economic order based on profit. What had he become if not an instrument to certify ownership in transactions aimed at making money? He established the bounds of farms about to change hands, laid out house lots to be offered the slow-growing population of the township, plotted new roads through the properties of enterprising real estate men, and more often than any other task, divided wood lots in preparation for their auction to lumber dealers. Frequent handling of old deeds and checking of old markers wore down his coating of indifference. "What's mine's my own," he mimicked in disgust, and exclaimed to himself, "How, when a man purchases a

---

[16] "Field Notes of Surveys Made by Henry D. Thoreau Since November, 1849," ms. in the Concord Free Public Library, by the kind permission of whose trustees it is used in this study. For Hubbard see Rebecca Wetherbee, "Memoir of Cyrus Hubbard," in *Memoirs of Members of the Social Circle in Concord, 2d Series, from 1795 to 1840* (Cambridge, Massachusetts, 1888), p. 192 f.

[17] "Field Notes of Surveys," p. 2.

[18] *Ibid.,* p. 3.

[19] John D. Gordan, "A Thoreau Handbill," *Bulletin of the New York Public Library,* LIX (May 1955), 253–58.

thing, he is determined to get and get hold of it, using how many expletives and how long a string of synonymous or similar terms signifying possession, in the legal process!" (VIII, 168)

Unlike the grinding of printer's graphite, his father's new trade,[20] which would have enclosed him in mill and shop and shielded him from its customers through business letters, surveying pushed Thoreau into association with the local farmers and entrepreneurs who were his employers. What he saw of their life—and more important, what he shared of it himself in the many hours of surveying—intensified his antagonism to the social order of which they were all a part and deepened the division between the two poles of his life pattern.

The best illustration of this educative function of his surveying is Thoreau's account of the verification of the bounds of Concord, in which he participated as an official representative, together with Selectmen of the bordering townships.[21] In prospect the perambulation of the bounds appealed to Thoreau as an activity which would yield whatever extramonetary values were to be had from surveying. For though its chief advantage to him lay in paying enough to enable a self-denying and thrifty bachelor to support himself and pay off his debts by working only part of the year and often only part of the day,

---

[20] Thoreau remained a surveyor the rest of his active life, the last entry in the "Field Notes of Surveys" being that for January 2, 1861, a few days after the lecture trip to Connecticut which is thought to have "brought on his final illness" (Walter Harding, "A Check List of Thoreau's Lectures," p. 87) and some four months before he journeyed to Minnesota in a vain search for improved health (XX, 339). But after has father fell ill, which was sometime in 1857 (XVII, 435), Thoreau also began to look after the family graphite business (Edward W. Emerson, *Henry Thoreau as Remembered by a Young Friend* [Boston and New York, 1917], p. 36 f.). Exactly when he took on this additional task has not yet been established, but it must have been before July 21, 1859, the date of a bill for graphite sent to the H. A. Lucas firm of Baltimore, whose reply of July 26 (now in the Houghton Library of Harvard University and cited by its permission) is the earliest business letter addressed directly to Thoreau that I have thus far uncovered.

[21] Another account of this incident is to be found in Hubert H. Hoeltje, "Thoreau in Concord Church and Town Records," *New England Quarterly*, XII (June 1939), 349–59.

he apparently expected by-products from an occupation which would keep him in the woods and open fields. It pleased him to remember that since the Concord roads radiated from the Center, the tour of the perimeter would cut across all of them, keeping his contact with these avenues of trade to a minimum, as if he had "undertaken to walk around the town at the greatest distance from its centre and at the same time from surrounding villages." It was to be "a sort of reconnoissance of its frontiers authorized by the central government of the town," which would "bring the surveyor in contact with whatever wild inhabitants or wilderness its territory embraces" (VIII, 498 f.). This in 1851 on the twelfth of September, with the perambulation three days off.

On the sixteenth, Thoreau described in his journal the inhabitants of the neighboring towns as they would be if one took their Selectmen as fair representatives. He tried to preserve his associates as he found them: Acton, "a mixture of quiet, respectable, and even gentlemanly farmer people, well to do in the world, with a rather boisterous, coarse, and a little self-willed class"; Bedford, "mechanics, who aspire to keep up with the age, with some of the polish of society, mingled with substantial and rather intelligent farmers" (IX, 3). Most interesting is the description of Sudbury. Years earlier in *A Week*, the young utopian had idealized the inhabitants of that up-river township as the yeomen of the preindustrial order: "rude and sturdy, experienced and wise men, keeping their castles, or teaming up their summer's wood, or chopping alone in the woods; men fuller of talk and rare adventure in the sun and wind and rain, than a chestnut is of meat, who were out not only in '75 and 1812, but have been out every day of their lives; greater men than Homer, or Chaucer, or Shakespeare, only they never got time to say so; they never took to the way of writing" (I, 6). In 1851: "farmers almost exclusively, exceedingly rough and countrified and more illiterate than usual, very tenacious of their rights and dignities and difficult to deal with" (IX, 3). The stubborn independence which had impressed him as a youth is still present, but in a context of reality rather than of myth.

As the perambulation went on and Thoreau found no wilderness or wild inhabitants but simply the typical men of the town walking on its outskirts, he turned this realistic vision upon them with still greater penetration. Among the representatives of Carlisle was one Isaiah Green, a man nearly eighty who had lived most of his days in an isolated part of the township which provided the preconditions for the solitude and intimacy with nature which Thoreau had sought on the shore of Walden. But what had his long life and similar lives amounted to? "Mere duration," judged Thoreau. "Here was the cider-mill, and there the orchard, and there the hog-pasture; and so men lived, and ate, and drank, and passed away,—like vermin." If only he could know "that he who resided here acted once in his life from a noble impulse, rising superior to his grovelling and penurious life, if only a single verse of poetry or of poetic prose had ever been written or spoken or conceived here beyond a doubt," he would "not think it in vain that man had lived here." But he found not one of these redeemers: "we only know that they ate, and drank, and built barns, and died and were buried"—and he exclaimed against this all-too-common emptiness, "That all his life he lived only as a farmer,—as the most valuable stock only on a farm,—and in no moments as a man!" (IX, 9–11)

The shock of seeing men thus reduced to anonymous functions of the economy led Thoreau to focus his examination on himself. He felt "inexpressibly begrimed," as if he had "committed suicide in a sense," and wrote, "My Pegasus has lost his wings; he has turned a reptile and gone on his belly" (IX, 5). The definition of bounds of ownership was impressing a similar deformation upon him too.

And now two reflex movements appeared in his journal entries on the perambulation. The first led toward denunciation of the social order of wasted humanity: "What can be uglier," he wondered, "than a country occupied by grovelling, coarse, and low-lived men? No scenery will redeem it" (IX, 23). The second sought for the opposite of such a society in the imagination: "The poet must keep himself unstained and aloof. Let him perambulate the bounds of Imagination's provinces, the realms of faery, and not the insignificant boundaries of towns. The excursions of the imagination are so boundless, the limits of towns are so petty" (IX, 5).

In the years when Thoreau surveyed for a living in the mornings and sought nourishment for his soul in the afternoons and evenings, it was these movements that dominated his thinking about the economic order; and it was chiefly from them that he derived this period's companion essays, "Life Without Principle," "Walking," and "Night and Moonlight."[22]

III

The distinguishing feature of the economic content of these essays is that it appears in two aspects, the one naturalistic, the other metaphorical. The typical economic writing of the communitarian experimenters—and Thoreau's when he was their individualistic counterpart—had been uniformly naturalistic: it presented with equally concrete detail both the industrial capitalism which it condemned from experience and the humanistic social order which it projected from imagination. After the failure of utopian experimentation, the criticism of existing society could continue unmodified. But the relict utopian who recognized this failure had perforce to abandon naturalism in his portrayal of the ideal. Thus Thoreau, continuing the critical description of Concord and America which had been logically preliminary to the Walden experiment, ceased to describe a social order suitable to essential human nature and, having again become a seeker

---

[22] The textual history of these essays remains to be established. The first two were prepared for publication while Thoreau lay on his deathbed in the early months of 1862 (Carl Bode, "Thoreau and his Last Publishers," *New England Quarterly*, XXVI (September 1953), 383–87). But the journal shows Thoreau actively engaged on "Walking" in the first two months of 1851 and on "Life Without Principle" just about a year later; and the former was first read as a lecture in April of 1851, the latter in November of 1854 (Harding, "A Check List of Thoreau's Lectures," pp. 82, 84). There is reason to believe, however, especially in the case of "Walking," that these lectures differed considerably from the present essays. "Night and Moonlight" (the title has no authority) was never prepared for publication by Thoreau and no one has established a single reliable text from the scattered manuscripts, portions of which have been published as "Night and Moonlight" (V, 323–33) and *The Moon* (Boston and New York, 1927). But it was delivered as a lecture on October 8, 1854 (Harding, "Check List," p. 83, and *Thoreau Society Bulletin* for April 1948), and all the identified journal passages used in its available components date from the early fifties.

for this social absolute, expressed in metaphor what was now beyond all other language.

The social criticism of this aspect of Thoreau's development, like its predecessor represented in the first chapter of *Walden,* did not start from necessity and human suffering but from freedom and human baseness. It supposed still that men lived a life they had chosen and that if they persisted in lying on their backs—as they seemed to him to be doing—it was because they made no effort to get up (IV, 461). Its stress, therefore, was not on the social order but on the individual, and its sympathy for the suffering of mankind was effectively hidden beneath a harsh tone of denunciation.

The starting point, as always, was Thoreau's own life and its reflections in the mirror of the township, which showed him his baser fraction exaggerated to become the totality of the lives of others. Looking still to an ideal in which the activities aimed at the unfolding of the soul would also yield a by-product to support the body—"as a steam planing-mill feeds its boilers with the shavings it makes" (IV, 461)—he found his own life and the lives of all others a failure. He could at least say for himself that he divided his energies and strove to minimize all expenditure that did not contribute to the growth and expression of his mind, but measured even by this lower standard, the lives of his townsmen were for the most part still failures. "We quarter our gross bodies on our poor souls," he said, somewhat of himself and chiefly of them, "till the former eat up all the latter's substance" (IV, 477). Divorced thus from a creative relationship with the mind, the life-consuming labors of the men of Concord became, in Thoreau's view, external and meaningless, contributing no more to man's development, as distinguished from the increase of his artifacts, than if they were reduced to "throwing stones over a wall" and "throwing them back" (IV, 457).

Nor were the rest of mankind anything more than his townsmen multiplied. Unable to describe an America he had never visited, Thoreau sought instead for its true symbol and found it in the Gold Rush. Openly a gamble while production for the market was only covertly so, obviously meaningless while the meaninglessness of other economic actions was masked by the usefulness of commodities, the Gold Rush seemed to Thoreau an extension and clarification of the evils he bore witness to in Concord. He knew of "no more startling development of the immorality of trade and all the common modes of getting a living (IV, 463). But especially did it demonstrate the debasement of a humanity that pursued simple acquisition as an end in itself.

After reading an "account of the Australian gold-diggings one evening" he had in his "mind's eye, all night, the numerous valleys, with their streams, all cut up with foul pits, from ten to one hundred feet deep, and half a dozen feet across, as close as they can be dug, and partly filled with water,—the locality to which men furiously rush to probe for their fortunes,—uncertain where they shall break ground,—not knowing but the gold is under their camp itself,—sometimes digging one hundred and sixty feet before they strike the vein, or then missing it by a foot,—turned into demons, and regardless of each other's rights, in their thirst for riches,—whole valleys, for thirty miles, suddenly honeycombed by the pits of the miners, so that even hundreds are drowned in them,—standing in water, and covered with mud and clay, they work night and day, dying of exposure and disease" (IV, 465).

Turning away in disgust from this vision of his contemporaries and himself—for it was the thought of his own "unsatisfactory life, doing as others do" (IV, 465), that had transformed a journalist's fact into the artist's image—Thoreau embarked on the voyage through the uncharted regions of his soul and the natural world which he took for its symbol. In "Walking" he provided this seeking with a manifesto, an extended metaphor skillfully wrought to fuse four separate aspects: Walks, the West, the Wild, and what he called Useful Ignorance.

The ground pattern of the metaphor, upon which the other themes are applied as overlay to create the density of his conception, lies in the compulsion which came upon Henry Thoreau every day to flee from compass, drawing table, house, street, stores, town, and to rid himself, if only for an hour, of all his "morning occupations" and "obligations to society" (V, 211), of the meaningless "work, work, work" and the "incessant business" (IV, 456) which he had denounced in "Life Without Principle." To escape from society and from the part of himself bartered to it for a living, he retreated into nature, "first along by the river, and then the brook, and then the meadow and the woodside" (V, 212), pacing toward that safe distance at which "church and state and school, trade and commerce and manufactures and agriculture, even politics," occupied but little space in the landscape (V, 212 f.). He avoided the highways, which led only to and from the economy he wished to abandon, and when he did not choose to go across lots limited himself to dirt paths, unused relics antedating plank and stone. For the economic order of Thoreau's afternoon was made up of vestiges of preindustrial New England. Sauntering on the Old Marlborough Road, whose mileposts seemed the gravestones of a dead commerce and industry, he met only lone-walking men who lived by ax and trap and fishline, the vagrants of Concord, whom he thought more of than he did its respected inhabitants.

But it was not apparent to Thoreau that his walks thus represented a motion backward. Concord Center lay north and east of the two river branches that joined near its main street, and when Thoreau, increasingly restricted by private appropriation of woodlands and meadows, sought out the streams and their lakelike expansions and narrow swampy valleys, he necessarily walked to the southwest and west: and he welcomed the coincidence between his own walks and the forward path of empire. For in westering, as in walking, he found a symbol of that sloughing off of inadequate old institutions and searching for new and better ones which was involved in his role as seeker. "We would fain take that walk," he wrote, "never yet taken by us through this actual world, which is perfectly symbolical of the path which we love to travel in the interior and ideal world" (V, 217). Even as he himself was turning away from what seemed an unredeemable degradation in America to seek a new and just absolute within the soul, so had the nations continually abandoned their unsuccessful civilizations to follow "the Great Western Pioneer," seeking ideals— perhaps "of vapor only"—beyond the sunset. "The island of Atlantis," he wrote, "and the islands and gardens of the Hesperides, a sort of terrestrial paradise, appear to have been the Great West of the ancients enveloped in mystery and poetry"; and who, he asked, "has not seen in imagination, when looking into the sunset sky, the gardens of the Hesperides, and the foundation of all those fables?" (V, 219.)

He did not delude himself with the thought that the colonizers of the West were then doing anything more than to transplant the East. When he wrote that he had to walk away from Europe it was toward Oregon, not California (V, 218). But he felt that if ever mankind left the Old World behind and created a new, it would be by moving away from what was finished and mapped and into the inchoate and unexplored—in the American West, perhaps, where the moon looked larger than in Europe, the heavens appeared higher, the stars brighter, "symbolical of the height to which the philosophy and poetry and religion of her inhabitants may one day soar" (V, 222). If men failed in this West, there was still the Pacific in which to drown the past—but the motion had always to be the same: "westward . . . with a spirit of enterprise and adventure" (V, 218). For the West which Thoreau had abstracted from his walking was itself the substratum of a still more abstract and general symbol, the Wild.

When he reached the Wild, Thoreau outdid himself in providing the reader with the "extreme statement" that had been promised him in the essay's first paragraph (V, 205). "Hope and the future for me are not in lawns and cultivated fields, not in towns and cities," he declared, "but in the impervious and quaking swamps," and "if it were proposed to me to dwell in the neighborhood of the most beautiful garden that ever human art contrived, or else of a Dismal Swamp, I should certainly decide for the swamp" (V, 226 f., 228). The meaning of his exaggerations he states less extravagantly after the first few have startled the reader into attention: "One who pressed forward incessantly and never rested from his labors, who grew fast and made infinite demands on life, would always find himself in a new country or wilderness, and surrounded by the raw material of life" (V, 226).

The Wild is whatever lies beyond the law already formulated, the institution already established, the pursued already overtaken. Its purpose is to be negated, to free man for the still wilder reach beyond it, and thus furnish its part toward his soul. It is not to be admired but to be conquered. "The bushwhack, the turf-cutter, the spade, and the bog hoe" (V, 230) are the weapons to be celebrated—whatever is useful in draining the wild swamps that lie out beyond our perimeter. So in literature, genius is "not a taper lighted at the hearth-stone of the race," a force tamed within convention and tradition, but "a light which makes the darkness visible" and "perchance shatters the temple of knowledge itself" (V, 231). Each man's mind, moreover, encloses a potential bit of this revolutionizing genius, his own "wild savage" (V, 237), which is the germ to be strengthened and liberated.

For society, writes Thoreau, adding the final tier to his structure, educates this pioneering intellect out of us and replaces it with insti-tution-preserving established knowledge. Quickly weaning the sav-age in our minds from "this vast, savage, howling mother of ours, Nature" (V, 237), it nourishes only that lesser portion which will speak the language and information that society approves of. But it is not just that the whole mind should be thus cultivated: there must be a frontier within to cope with the frontier without. Above the "Useful Knowledge" acceptable to society is "Useful Ignorance": a "Sympathy with Intelligence" which accompanies our "novel and grand surprise on a sudden revelation of the insufficiency of all that we called Knowledge before" (V, 239 f.). It is by means of this Useful Ignorance that the mind liberates itself from the past and opens the way to the conquest of the wild residue in the universe which will ever be beyond our capture.

Applied externally to the physical world, to society, and to the operations of the mind, Thoreau's manifesto must waken all who would advance thought and through it rescue men and women from the debasement which he urged us to struggle against. But it was not in this manner that Thoreau applied it to himself in the aspect of his life which we are here examining. Looking only into his own thoughts—for all he read in nature was simply himself projected—he found at best but a metaphorical achievement of an ideal which had already failed in reality and at worst a yearning and frustration. The conclusion of "Walking," which urges us to persevere in the search till one day the sun will "light up our whole lives with a great awakening light" (V, 248), is but a weak echo of the impassioned optimism at the end of *Walden,* as if affected by the confession which precedes it: "Unto a life which I call natural I would gladly follow even a will-o'-the-wisp through bogs and sloughs unimaginable, but no moon nor firefly has shown me the causeway to it" (V, 242).

It is significant that he refers his failure thus to moon and firefly, for as the ideal life escaped him in days increasingly divided between surveying and science, one as much a servant of the profit economy as the other, Thoreau came to believe that he might seize and hold it by moonlight. "That kind of life," he wrote, "which, sleeping, we dream that we live awake, in our walks by night, we, waking, live, while our daily life appears as a dream" (VIII, 496).

The world of Thoreau's moonlight has no economy. There is neither "Business, with his four prime ministers Trade and Commerce and Manufactures and Agriculture" (VIII, 378), nor any relics of preindustrial New England to evolve into Business. Nevertheless the effect of a just economy is evidenced in the night's "primeval simplicity" (IX, 264). The elimination of details from the landscape creates the same precondition for self-culture as the elimination of indirect economic processes from society: "We are not oppressed by their multitude but can erect ourselves."[23]

It is a world of nature rather than of men. Each evening "night surely repossesses herself of her realms," and Thoreau can walk out "as if into a scenery anciently inhabited by men but now deserted by them."[24] But consistent with the fact that Thoreau's science was chiefly economic botany, an adjunct of profit-directed agriculture, it is nature in darkness, with its inhabitants denied the use of such a science's primary instruments.

The symbol of this world's oversoul is the moon. Thoreau had from his youth represented oversoul by the sun and sunlight. In *The Service,* for example, he had spoken of evil as the shadow created by men's resistance to the goodness of the universe—"the light of the System"—and had urged that our lives so correspond with the oversoul that we might be said to live with minimal shadow, "under the equator, with the sun in the meridian."[25] And in *Walden* he had proclaimed, "There is more day to dawn. The sun is but a morning

---

[23] *The Moon,* p. 37.

[24] *Ibid.,* p. 50.

[25] Ed. F. B. Sanborn (Boston, 1902), p. 8.

star" (II, 367).[26] Here he speaks as if the unholy activities which the sun lights and thus figuratively sanctions have perhaps sullied its symbolism. The dawn is still pure, "unfallen day" (VIII, 503), but the working hours are day defiled, and it is only at evening, when "perchance some impurity has begun to sink to earth strained by the air" (XI, 186 f.), that the sun's light begins to regain the symbolic power which is to reach its height only by reflection in the moon. The moon is identified with the soul, especially with the soul of an uncertain seeker no longer confident that he can approach the absolute frontally. Her light is "sufficient . . . for the pensive walker, and not disproportionate to the inner light we have" (IX, 8).

The landscape which this moon lights up is that of the primitive world in which life is still close to bare essentials. It is associated in Thoreau's mind with Ossian (XIII, 11), with the Indian (XIII, 20), and with the Maine woods. "Fair Haven pond by moonlight," he writes, "lies there like a lake in the Maine wilderness in the midst of a primitive forest untrodden by man. This light and this hour take the civilization all out of the landscape" (VIII, 464).

Thoreau's moonlight world thus satisfied the prerequisites for that highest life of the senses which was involved when he asked if we could not *see* God. For a concentrated moment it allowed him to feel free of the debasing effect of the economy, seemed to place him, alone, in immediate contact with a primitive and undefiled nature, and so appeared to grant his higher instincts unobstructed access to the spiritual order which he believed to be enclosed within inert and living matter. If his eyes were denied him, his other senses were sharpened. His ear could more readily detect the general earth song when all individual sounds had subsided, his nostrils distinguish the underlying scent of the world's earthiness. All was in readiness for what he described, in his phase of seeking, as his "profession": "to be always on the alert to find God in nature, to know his lurking-places, to attend all the oratorios, the operas, in nature" (VIII, 472). He discovered nothing, however, but what has been described: a utopian

---

[26] An analysis of the sun imagery in *Walden* is to be found in John G. Broderick, "Imagery in *Walden*," *University of Texas Studies in English,* XXXIII (1954), 80–89.

inversion of reality, bypassing the social order and momentarily creating a successful Walden life in the realm of the wish. To discover any other ideal was beyond the methods available to him.

IV

It is not by mere coincidence that the remarkable journal entry which includes the definition of Thoreau's aim as seeker also includes sentences used in "Life Without Principle" to condemn the social order. For as has already been argued, what Thoreau opposed to acquisitive society in this phase was not a different kind of society but an individual life devoted to the search for its postulates in the absolute of soul and nature. "I am convinced that men are not well employed, that this is not the way to spend a day," he writes—and adds immediately: "If by patience, if by watching, I can secure one new ray of light, can feel myself elevated for an instant upon Pisgah, the world which was dead prose to me becoming living and divine . . . shall I not be a watchman henceforth? If by watching a whole year on the city's walls I may obtain a communication from heaven, shall I not do well to shut up my shop and turn a watchman?" (VIII, 471)

Thoreau's contact with the absolute was to be an experience from which he would bring back ideas to be incorporated in his life and writing.[27] Two passages in the journal entry we have been quoting from deal with these presumably extrasocietal cognitions.

"What if one moon has come and gone with its world of poetry, its weird teachings, its oracular suggestions?" asks the first. "Suppose you attend to the hints, to the suggestions, which the moon makes for one month, . . . will they not be very different from anything in literature or religion or philosophy?" (VIII, 470) Remembering the moon's function as the substitute symbol of oversoul, we can see that this question is generically identical with another which Thoreau had asked himself six years earlier at the pond: "What if we were to obey these fine dictates, these divine suggestions, which are ad-

---

[27] For another development of this idea see Sherman Paul, "The Wise Silence: Sound as the Agency of Correspondence in Thoreau," *New England Quarterly*, XXII (December 1949), 511–27.

dressed to the mind and not to the body, which are certainly true,—not to eat meat, not to buy, or sell, or barter, etc., etc., etc.?" (VIII, 382) Contact with the moon was contact with the changing but continually just morality of the oversoul which man should always be striving to catch up with.

Similarly in the second passage, Thoreau says of "ecstatic states" that while they cannot be contemporary with their expression, they provide resources for "calmer seasons," constituting an "experience of infinite beauty on which we unfailingly draw, which enables us to exaggerate ever truly" (VIII, 468 f.). What Thoreau called exaggeration was his technique for trying to express the truth which directed practice but had not yet been fully attained by it. "We live by exaggeration," he had declared in his article on Carlyle; "what else is it to anticipate more than we enjoy?" (IV, 353) So also in *Walden* when prescribing the search for the absolute: "Who that has heard a strain of music feared then lest he should speak extravagantly any more forever? ... The volatile truth of our words should continually betray the inadequacy of the residual statement" (II, 357).

What these passages suggest is that Thoreau's correspondence with the oversoul in nature is not to be separated from the cognitions about ideal man and ideal society which he expected to achieve through it. The long and apparently unfinished history of the appeal to natural law has surely demonstrated that nature, like deity of any sort, will seem to reflect to the observer whatever extrabiological belief he projects into it. The younger Thoreau made use of nature as a vehicle by which to find sanction for economic views and practices which had their origin not in nature but among men. That he resorted to this fanciful epistemology reflects only the fact that the social self-interest of groups of men expresses itself not simply in knowledge but in the ways by which knowledge is believed to have been discovered. The rejection of all the evolutionary paths within the possibilities of society as it exists, the search for an ideal pattern "outside" society (that is, in nature) to which men can then conform, the seeming employment in this search of an epistemology which bases itself on nature and which differs from the epistemologies employed by other social groups to arrive at other conclusions, the discovery of a pattern which is an idealization of the preindustrial economy: what are these but the interdependent elements of a single complex of ideas? The breakdown of the social experiment at Walden involved not simply the economic pattern but the entire complex of which it was a part, and it is therefore not surprising that in the critical years after the return from the pond the failure to discover a new social absolute through correspondence is accompanied by failure to achieve correspondence itself.

At times Thoreau expresses this failure in an exclamation of yearning: "Oh, if I could be intoxicated on air and water! on hope and memory! and always see the maples standing red in the midst of the waters on the meadow!" (VIII, 72) More poignant, however, are the statements which mingle cold self-observation with his feelings. Now, he writes in midsummer of 1851, "many sounds and sights only remind me that they once said something to me, and are so by association interesting. I go forth to be reminded of a previous state of existence, if perchance any memento of it is to be met with hereabouts" (VIII, 302 f.). The day of the vernal equinox in 1853 he is affected by the warmth of the wind and the softness of the air and sits down by a wall "to see if I can muse again." For a moment there is promise of success: frost seems to be melting out of him, "thoughts like a freshet pour down unwonted channels," a sound of music shows him "petty men" as "the shadows of grander to come," the roads seem to lead "elsewhither than to Carlisle and Sudbury." "Encouraged," he writes, "I set out once more to climb the mountain of the earth, for my steps are symbolical steps, and in all my walking I have not reached the top of the earth yet." But he gets no nearer to it that day. When he hears the peep of a frog he asks, still hopefully, "If the hyla has revived again, may not I?" But when he sits down to write in his journal, the day's failure is not quite hidden by the stubborn courage with which he resolves to try once again: "life is a battle in which you are to show your pluck, and woe be to the coward. . . . Despair and postponement are cowardice and defeat. Men were born to succeed, not to fail" (XI, 34–36).

In his attempts to understand what was happening to him, Thoreau fell back on the belief that the ability to achieve correspondence with nature was a quality of youth and that he had lost it because he was no longer young. "My life was ecstasy," he wrote in the most successful expression of this feeling. "In youth before I lost any of my senses, I can remember that I was all alive, and inhabited my body with inexpressible satisfaction; both its weariness and its refreshment were sweet to me. This earth was the most glorious musical instrument, and I was audience to its strains" (VIII, 306 f.).

The rest of the explanation he hinted at himself toward the end of 1859, when the period of his most intense regret was over. Before middle age, he suggests, a man still trails the clouds of glory: he seems to be allied "to a noble race of beings, to whom he in part belongs, or with whom he is in communication." "Prompted by the reminiscence of that other sphere from which he so lately arrived, his actions are unintelligible to his seniors" and "he really thinks and talks about a larger sphere of existence than this world. It takes him forty years to accommodate himself to the carapax of this world. This is the age of poetry. Afterward he may be the president of a bank and go the way of all flesh" (XIX, 35).

The most significant element here is the echo of Wordsworth. What the period of the French Revolution had been to Wordsworth, the period of the reform movement was to Thoreau. Both men had been granted the accident of a youth coincident with a time of social upheaval in which the common mind breaks out of institution-preserving bounds, and each had shared in its liberation. For both as well, the period of upheaval failed to yield the goals expected of it, and each then moved on toward an older self different from his youth, seeing the latter's glories more and more brightly as they receded.

The failure of Thoreau's ability to achieve correspondence represents only one aspect of the change that was taking place in him. The other was the motion toward a new synthesis, which, as has been said, developed between the poles of the life pattern of the morning surveyor and the afternoon seeker.

In the midst of his regrets about the loss of youth, Thoreau looked forward to new triumphs in maturity. "The youth," he wrote, "gets together his materials to build a bridge to the moon, or perchance a palace or temple on the earth, and at length the middle-aged man concludes to build a woodshed with them." But he recovered himself immediately and added the following: "Trees have commonly two growths in the year, a spring and a fall growth, the latter sometimes equalling the former, and you can see where the first was checked whether by cold or drouth . . . So is it with men; most have a spring growth only, and never get over this first check to their youthful hopes; but plants of hardier constitution, or perchance planted in a more genial soil, speedily recover themselves, and, though they bear the scar or knot in remembrance of their disappointment, they push forward again and have a vigorous fall growth which is equivalent to a new spring" (X, 227 f.).

3

The Union of Principle and Expediency

The view of society toward which Thoreau advanced after the testing at Walden was the ideological counterpart of his surveying—that is to say, it was founded on the acceptance of industrial capitalism as impersonally dictated necessity and it performed functions useful within that social order. It made an amalgam, however, with the high ideals which had motivated Thoreau's practice as a utopian. Consequently, it was for the most part a philosophy of social reform, attempting to ameliorate the condition of mankind without changing the principles underlying the social structure. But it included a different element as well: ideals which Thoreau was unable to combine with the self-interest of any group in his society and which therefore never developed their strategy. Whatever its successes, this social philosophy could not escape an undertone of frustration.

It is a peculiarity of Thoreau's intellectual history that the evolution of this view of society proceeds unevenly along three lines, each unusually independent of the others. His economic botany, for example, attains success because it goes beyond individual plants to deal with the biological community, but he does not apply this ability to think in terms of social organism to the human community. Again, he concludes that private property is a mistaken policy and calls for a degree of public ownership in parks and river banks, but he does not apply this principle elsewhere in the economy. His social thought moves along complementary lines in relation to nature, Northern capitalism, and Southern slavery; he never fuses the three aspects into a whole.

I

Thoreau's early approach to nature (as has already been argued in this study) had contained two antagonistic elements. The first, its limit mysticism, was associated with the utopian phase of his opposition to the economic order. The second, its limit pure science, expressed that aspect of his personality which spontaneously accepted this order. During the years at Walden, when this polarity first became undeniably evident, the second element was carried in Thoreau's investigations of the pond, and these studies he continued and extended in his remaining years.[1] But as the vehicle for his general intellectual development they were succeeded by his research in forestry.

Thoreau's investigation of forest trees began, as did his scientific botany in general, about 1850 (XV, 157), during the period when his approach to nature was still dominated by the search for an extrasocietal ideal. It is not surprising, therefore, that he can be observed projecting into trees the characteristics of the utopian order and of the heroic aspirant man about whom it was to have centered. Idealization of the tree at the expense of man, combined with regret for a lost youth and with yearning for a society not to be found in industrializing America, is threaded all through the journals of the eighteen-fifties.

At the end of 1851, for example, Thoreau watched from a hillside while two men cut down a pine below. The tree "towered up a hundred feet . . . one of the tallest probably in the township and straight as an arrow," aspiring to perfection as should each man, and it fell "as softly as a feather, folding its green mantle about it like a warrior, as if, tired of standing, it embraced the earth with silent joy, returning its elements to the dust again." Those who had felled it were "diminutive manikins," gnawing through its bole "like beavers or insects"

---

[1] For an account of Thoreau's study of limnology, see Edward S. Deevey, Jr., "A Re-examination of The reau's *Walden*," *Quarterly Journal of Biology*, XVII (March 1942), 1–11.

(IX, 162 f.). The pine, wrote Thoreau a few month later, "seems the emblem of my life; it stands for the west, the wild" (IX, 452).

The best example of this projection, witnessing the persistence of the unrewarded seeker, occurs in the first days of 1856, when there was cut down on the Boston Road in Concord a venerable elm whose rings showed it to have sprung up some one hundred and thirty years earlier, a half-century before the township fired its rifles against the British. Thoreau had first measured this tree—the Davis Elm—in 1852 (X, 90). When it began to creak in the winter storms three years later and Mrs. Davis feared for her roof, he visited daily to watch the preparations for the felling. He looked into his histories and botanies for descriptions of other giants of the species and compared this tree in his journal with the surviving notable elms of Concord. To a Thoreau increasingly aware of his own aging and changing, the great elm represented the lost preindustrial township whose idealization had been an element in his lost youth. "Another link that bound us to the past is broken," he exclaimed. "It has passed away together with the clergy of the old school and the stage-coach which used to rattle beneath it. . . . How much of old Concord falls with it!" (XIV, 131)

In the elms he recovered symbolically the human heroes who had long been absent from his native town: not the hacks of political parties, but the nonjoining men of principle whom he once thought to have glimpsed in Nathaniel Peabody Rogers. "They attend no caucus," he wrote shortly after the felling of the Davis Elm, "they make no compromise, they use no policy. Their one principle is growth. They combine a true radicalism with a true conservatism. Their radicalism is not cutting away of roots, but an infinite multiplication and extension of them under all surrounding institutions. They take a firmer hold on the earth that they may rise higher into the heavens. . . . Their conservatism is a dead but solid heartwood, which is the pivot and firm column of support to all this growth, appropriating nothing to itself, but forever by its support assisting to extend the area of their radicalism. Half a century after they are dead at the core, they are preserved by radical reforms" (XIV, 140 f.).

Standing within the Thoreau who composed these sentimental epitaphs on an idealism beyond his practice was the man who surveyed wood lots for auction to lumber dealers and calculated their yield in salable cords. After the woodcutters had felled the pine, Thoreau went down into the valley and estimated it: "It was about four feet in diameter where it was sawed, about one hundred feet long" (IX, 163). The venerable elm too he looked at with his other, his commercial eye: "Supposing the first fifteen feet to average six feet in diameter, they would contain more than three cords and a foot of wood, but probably not more than three cords" (XIV, 132).

Thoreau thus witnessed the accelerating destruction of New England's forests from contradictory aspects. The indispensability of nature to a just man striving for self-culture rather than profit he had long accepted as an absolute principle. But to begin with, he had so far yielded to expediency as to become an important instrument in the very destruction which he necessarily regretted. The first survey recorded in his "Field Notes" was the division of Isaac Watts's woodland,[2] where twenty-five years earlier, as a child unconsciously absorbing the influences of nature, he had "played horse in the paths of a thick wood and roasted apples and potatoes in an old pigeon-place and gathered fruit at the pie-apple tree" (VIII, 88). Shortly after he laid them out the lots were auctioned, and then the trees were cut down. And one after another in the early fifties, alternating with house lots and farms and an occasional road and once even a design for a machine, the surveys of woodland appear in his record: Ralph Waldo Emerson's lot in March of 1850, Cyrus Stow's the same month, a second of Emerson's in October, three for Nathan Brooks, Cyrus Stow again, and James B. Wood in November; in 1851 two more for Cyrus Stow and single lots for John Hosmer, Reuben Brown, and Samuel Barrett—a new element making itself felt in his relation to the forest.[3] "To-day," he writes in 1850 of a field where he had once

---

[2] "Field Notes of Surveys," p. 1.

[3] The rest of the record may be found in the "Field Notes of Surveys," where all the surveys mentioned here are listed. Thoreau completed a plan of a "lead-pipe machine" for George Loring on September 15, 1852, charging him twelve dollars and apparently receiving only five (Field Notes, pp. 87, 149). What appears to be a sketch of this machine is now in the Concord Free Public Library on a sheet later used in the January 1853 survey of the land of John Le Grosse.

been blackberrying, "I was aware that I walked in a pitch pine wood, which ere long, perchance, I may survey and lot off for a wood auction" (VIII, 89).

Nor did Thoreau view his role as a destructive agent wholly with aversion. He protested vigorously against the deforestation of his native Middlesex County, exclaiming in one place, "The very willow-rows lopped every three years for fuel or powder, and every sizable pine and oak, or other forest tree, cut down within the memory of man! As if individual speculators were to be allowed to export the clouds out of the sky, or the stars out of the firmament, one by one."[4] What is perhaps more significant, he pondered the evil effects of this deforestation on his own life and by implication on the lives of others. Once in 1850 he considers this problem symbolically, writing of "simple brooks" which were dammed up and thus "taught to use their influence to destroy the primitive forests on their borders" and which now "for penalty . . . flow in shrunken channels" (VIII, 82). Two years later he is more explicitly personal. "The woods I walked in in my youth are cut off," he writes. "Is it not time that I ceased to sing?" (IX, 345 f.).

But this same year brings a question of an opposite order: "These woods! Why do I not feel their being cut more sorely? Does it not affect me nearly?" (IX, 224) And although he goes on to say, "I shall go to Walden less frequently," he is unable to hold to his resolution. Not a week later he walks to the pond again, seeking a compensation for the lost woodland. Earlier he had visited the hill on which Watts's trees had once stood and found it "a pleasant surprise . . . to see, instead of dense ranks of trees almost impermeable to light, distant well-known blue mountains in the horizon and a . . . white village over an expanded open country" (VIII, 88). So now he finds that though the Walden woods are being cut off, it is "not all loss," for it makes "some new and unexpected prospects" (IX, 253).

Among these prospects was the sight of the woodcutters: "the log-

---

[4] This passage is from "Chesuncook" (III, 170) and was thus not published until 1858, but I have assumed that it represents a sentiment of 1853, the year of the trip to Maine described in that essay. The "powder" is a reference to the use of willows at the Acton powder mill, for a record of which see VIII, 410.

ger's team, his oxen on the ice chewing the cud, the long pine tree, stripped of its branches, chained upon his sled, resting on a stout cross-bar or log and trailing behind, the smoke of his fire curling up blue amid the trees, the sound of the axe and of the teamsters' voices" (IX, 253). Despite his love of the forest and his desire to see it preserved, Thoreau was drawn extraordinarily to the woodcutter and the lumberer. It was an old attraction going back at least as far as the Walden years, when he was celebrating that "true Homeric" man the wood-chopper Therien (II, 159), an element of the general tug of the primitive which the younger Thoreau had felt so intensely and which the older man never entirely lost. What especially satisfied him as he observed the felling of the Walden woods was that it brought to Concord—barely over the horizon from metropolitan Boston—the wild flavor of Maine and New Hampshire (IX, 253).

When Thoreau in 1853 voyaged to Maine for the second time, he fell in with men whose job was to find cuttable timber, and in "Chesuncook" he described their "solitary and adventurous life" with relish: "They search for timber over a given section, climbing hills and often high trees to look off; explore the streams by which it is to be driven, and the like; spend five or six weeks in the woods, they two alone, a hundred miles or more from any town, roaming about, and sleeping on the ground where night overtakes them, depending chiefly on the provisions they carry with them, though they do not decline what game they come across. . . . They work ever with a gun as well as an axe, let their beards grow, and live without neighbors . . . far within a wilderness."

The life he was thus drawn to was that of men who participated in the ravaging of the forests, and Thoreau tried to confront its evil consequences by ending his essay with a plea for conservation. But there remained the echo of the counterpoint: "I have often wished since that I was with them" (III, 112).

The significance of Thoreau's silvical investigations is that they led to a reconciliation of these contradictory strains in his attitude to the forest. His discovery of the mechanism of succession pointed to a system of forest management which would yield lumber and profit to satisfy man's grosser instincts and at the same time preserve nature for the disciplining of his spirit.

II

The succession of forest trees had been observed by New Englanders for many years before Henry Thoreau became a botanist. As far back as 1796 the Rev. Timothy Dwight (later to become president of Yale University) traversed in one of his many journeys a plain of yellow pines over part of which these trees had been cut down and succeeded by oaks. "Such a change in forest vegetation is not uncommon," he noted, "and will hereafter be made a subject of inquiry"[5]— and so in time it was.

Dwight himself knew that the spontaneous succession which he had observed could be the means for making the New England forests, as he expressed it, "in a sense ever-living."[6] For he had noticed, or perhaps read somewhere, that the forest floor itself provided optimum conditions for the germination and growth of the seeds of forest trees. These seeds would not do well on a sunlit field or if planted in earth. Covered by the fallen leaves, however, they were not only sheltered from hungry rodents but were allowed to rest on the surface of a loose, light, water-holding soil and to spring up under the protecting shade of the woodland. "In this manner, and by a process totally superior to any contrived by the human mind," concluded the pious Dwight, "forests are furnished by the Author of nature with the means of perpetual self-restoration."[7]

The conditions which would encourage research in natural succession were not present, however, in Dwight's America. In 1795 the Society of Arts and Manufactures in the State of New York did indeed publish a report on the "best mode of preserving and increasing the growth of timber."[8] But more typical was the discussion of forest lands in Tench Coxe's *A View of the United States of America,* issued a year earlier.[9] Although Coxe was sufficiently foresighted to warn

---

[5] *Travels in New-England and New-York* (4 vols., London, 1823), I, 270.

[6] *Ibid.,* I, 81.

[7] *Ibid.,* I, 80.

[8] Quoted in Bernhard E. Fernow, *A Brief History of Forestry in Europe, the United States and Other Countries* (Toronto, 1907), p. 402.

[9] (Philadelphia, 1794), pp. 450–57.

that it would be unwise for Americans to "neglect the due preservation of their timber,"[10] his chief concern was to show how their vast forests might be used to supply exports to Europe and thus earn money for investment in industry while at the same time freeing more earth for farming. Instead of rules for conservation, he therefore provided his readers with instructions on how to clear forest lands and with lists of the manufactures employing wood.

Even as late as 1851, a writer in a government report on agriculture apologized for discussing French attempts to use fertilizers in forests with the remark that this question had an interest in France which could "hardly be understood in America," where the difficulty was "rather to clear the ground of its woody growth than to stimulate it to greater fruitfulness."[11]

The successive availability of great wooded regions in the West, combined with the development of railroads to transport lumber from forest and mill, kept silviculture from being a national concern in our country until near the end of the nineteenth century.[12]

That Henry Thoreau (among others) thus anticipated national developments by several decades was due first of all to his being so much a New Englander. The deforestation whose economic effect is the parent of silviculture was in the normal course of events felt first in the region where towns and industries had existed longest. Thoreau's surveying gave him a vantage point from which he could hardly fail to notice it, and his belief in man's need for nature, combined with a commercial instinct educated in the wood-using pencil manufacture, heightened the sensitivity of his observation. It was this foundation, involving both his livelihood and philosophy, that made it possible for him to use his knowledge of biology in order to arrive at an understanding of the mechanism of succession.

Like other biologists of his day, Thoreau was interested in the significance of the distribution of plants and animals and in the rele-

---

[10] *Ibid.,* p. 457.

[11] "Cultivating Forests," in *Report of the Commissioner of Patents for the Year 1851, Part II: Agriculture* (Washington, D.C., 1852), p. 53.

[12] Fernow, *Brief History of Forestry*, p. 403. Herbert A. Smith, "The Early Forestry Movement in the United States," *Agricultural History*, XII (October 1938), 326.

vant subject of the dispersion of seeds. As early as the summer of 1850, when his disciplined study of botany was just beginning (XV, 157), he remarked on a little pitch pine which grew in his yard although he did not know of another such tree "within half a mile" (VIII, 41). The following year he began to pay careful attention to the methods by which the seed of such a tree might have been planted.

In May he was reading about Jimson weed in a materia medica but, instead of noting down its medicinal properties, copied into his journal the quotation that it "emigrates with great facility, and often springs up in the ballast of ships, and in earth carried from one country to another" (VIII, 219). Two months later, finding the plant on the Massachusetts seacoast, he felt as if he was "on the highway of the world, at sight of this cosmopolite and veteran traveller" (VIII, 343). Back in Concord in the fall he noticed "the downy seeds of the groundsel . . . taking their flight" (VIII, 490), picked the barbed beggar-ticks from his clothing (IX, 65), and freed the dense-packed milkweed seeds to watch their graceful voyaging (IX, 17–23). "By all methods," he wrote, nature distributes plants, "whether by the balloon, or parachute, or hook, or barbed spear . . . or mere lightness which the winds can waft" (IX, 65).

Thoreau did not realize at this time that there was a connection between the dispersion of seed and the succession of forests. He was perhaps dimly aware of the latter, for he began to count rings on the stumps of great trees as if to reconstruct the primitive woodland which had almost entirely vanished from Concord, and he remarked at one point, "How foreign is the yellow pine to the green woods"— and asked, "What business has it here?" (VIII, 29) But his perception was limited by the accepted opinion that the way to produce mature forests was to plant them from seed. Thus in the fall of 1851 he noticed a few of the primitive oaks in a pasture ("great ornaments" he thought them), noticed too that no young oaks were replacing them, and wondered if there would be any a century later, but concluded, "One day they will be planted, methinks, and nature reinstated to some extent" (VIII, 461 f.).

In April of 1852 Thoreau still talked of planting forests, but now in connection with an observation which was to lead in a new direction. He noticed that recently-fallen acorns lying among the dead leaves had been sprouting, the rootlet "already turning toward the bowels of the earth, already thinking of the tempests which it is destined as an oak to withstand, if it escapes worm and squirrel." If you would "make a forest," he advised, "pick these up and plant them" (IX, 481).

Eight months later Thoreau observed the sprouting of chestnuts under similar conditions and realized that he had learned how new forests are planted by nature. The nuts which had fallen that year were already "partially mixed with the mould, as it were, under the decaying and mouldy leaves," where they had "all the moisture and manure" they needed and were "concealed from squirrels" (X, 434 f.). Having thus established for himself what Timothy Dwight had known at least a generation earlier, Thoreau had now to determine why it was that the seeds which sprouted successfully in a forest were not those which had fallen from its trees but were of different species that might be growing only at a distance.

Early in 1853, continuing his study of the dissemination of chestnuts, he found little piles of these nuts near the galleries of meadow mice. By March he was ready to conclude that mice and squirrels stored many nuts away in "secure, sufficiently dry and sufficiently moist places" (XI, 9) to allow them to sprout and that thus "new groves of chestnuts" were being born (XI, 30). After "chestnuts" Thoreau added in parentheses the query "and of oaks?" He knew then that what he had learned about chestnuts might also be true of these other species, which are involved in succession patterns with pines and which were among those which Thoreau wished to have preserved.

For almost three years Thoreau allowed this knowledge to rest in his mind and journal unexploited. He continued to be interested in the dispersion of seed, particularly in the way squirrels cut down pine cones and opened their scales.[13] He also observed with a regret that now approached anguish the accelerating destruction of Concord's remaining forests. "Our woods," he wrote in early spring of 1855, "are now so reduced that the chopping of this winter has been a cutting to the quick" (XIII, 231). And in December: "Now I hear,

[13] XIII, 214, 227 f., 447.

half a mile off, the hollow sound of woodchopping, the work of short winter days begun, which is gradually laying bare and impoverishing our landscape. In two or three thicker woods which I have visited this season, I was driven away by this ominous sound" (XIV, 48).

On April 28, 1856, the hitherto unrelated pieces of information lying dormant in Thoreau's mind were precipitated into a synthesis. The immediate impulse, preserved in the journal, was a comment by a man who seems to have been helping Thoreau survey a farm.[14] "Observing the young pitch pines by the road south of Loring's lot that was so heavily wooded, George Hubbard remarked that if they were cut down oaks would spring up, and sure enough, looking across the road to where Loring's white pines recently stood so densely, the ground was all covered with oaks." His mind alerted, Thoreau immediately instructed himself in his journal to "look at the site of some thick pine woods which I remember"—woods which he had very likely surveyed for cutting himself—"and see what has sprung up" (XIV, 315). Some ten days later he recorded one such observation which confirmed Hubbard's remark (XIV, 329), and before another week had passed he formulated an hypothesis to explain what he had seen.

If after a dense pine wood is cut down the trees which spring up are not pine but oak and other hardwoods, it is because the seeds of these hardwoods have been transported to the pines from distant groves by animals and have sprouted under their shade, ready to shoot up when the pines are felled. It may appear to some that the acorns must have lain dormant in the soil since the day that this land had been occupied by oaks, "but if you look through a thick pine wood," wrote Thoreau, "you will detect many little oaks, birches, etc., sprung probably from seeds carried into the thicket by squirrels, etc., and blown thither, but which are overshadowed and choked by the pines. This planting under the shelter of the pines may be carried on annually, and the plants annually die, but when the pines are cleared off, the oaks, etc., having got just the start they want, and now secured favorable conditions, immediately spring up to trees" (XIV, 334 f.).

---

[14] On this day Thoreau was surveying for Samuel Staples, the constable who had jailed him in 1846 ("Field Notes of Surveys," p. 106).

Thoreau did not seriously test this hypothesis until September 24, 1857. That morning he noticed a squirrel burying something under a hemlock, and digging after the animal found two hickory nuts under about an inch and a half of soil. "This, then," he wrote, reaffirming his conclusion of 1853, "is the way forests are planted. This nut must have been brought twenty rods at least and was buried at just the right depth. If the squirrel is killed, or neglects its deposit, a hickory springs up" (XVI, 40). That afternoon, incited by this incident perhaps, Thoreau visited a "very dense and handsome white pine grove" and found on its floor, "as often as every five feet, a little oak, three to twelve inches high." "I was surprised," he confessed to himself, "to find my own theory so perfectly proved" (XVI, 40 f.).

It was this theory, supported more firmly by other observations, that Thoreau presented to an audience of Middlesex County farmers on September 20, 1860, in his lecture "The Succession of Forest Trees." The only element in it new to science—and he claimed no more—was that which derived from Thoreau's studies of the dispersion of seed. The other essential components had already been described by the botanist George B. Emerson in 1846.[15]

In the development of Thoreau's social philosophy, this explanation of the mechanism of succession was important less for itself than for its consequences. Immediately after Thoreau formulated his hypothesis in 1856, he recorded a conversation which shows him to have been thinking about the implications of an understanding of succession for the management of wood lots. He had been speaking to the successful farmer John Hosmer about the wood lot pointed out by Hubbard, on which the pines were being succeeded by shrub oak, an economically useless growth. Hosmer's opinion was that its new owner would never see "any decent wood there as long as he lives." But he went on to tell Thoreau about a similar experience of his own whose significance he perhaps did not fully understand. He had had "a lot of pine in Sudbury, which being cut, shrub oak came up. He cut and burned and raised rye, and the next year (it being surrounded by pine woods on three sides) a dense growth of pine sprang up."

---

[15] *A Report on the Trees and Shrubs Growing Naturally in the Forests of Massachusetts* (Boston, 1846), pp. 19, 28–30.

What Hosmer had done without prevision was to take advantage of the mechanism of succession to get a growth of salable pine instead of profitless shrub oak. "If you cut the shrub oak soon," generalized Thoreau, "probably pines or birches, maples or other trees which have light seeds, will spring next, because squirrels, etc., will not be likely to carry acorns into open land" (XIV, 363).

By 1856, then, Thoreau had groped his way to the threshold of a fundamentally modern forestry, which, as a recent authority has stated, is "primarily a matter of continuous management of existing forests, with dependence chiefly on natural reproduction, not tree planting, for replacement of the stand."[16] Using his knowledge of the natural laws of the forest community, Thoreau saw the possibility of a management which would both encourage the growth of profitable timber and minimize the time during which forest land was not covered by trees. In the period of intense labor which followed his lecture on succession and which was cut short only by the onset of his fatal illness, Henry Thoreau systematically investigated the forest on the basis of this principle.[17]

One line of his research sought to deepen his understanding of the different patterns of succession. He turned from the pine-oak sequence to study the succession of white pines to pitch pines.[18] Moreover, since his pure pine wood succeeded by pure oak was an abstraction from which actual forests differed owing both to natural complexities and the unplanned management of their owners, Thoreau began to acquaint himself with the ways in which succession took place in woods of mixed species and uneven densities.[19]

Related to this subject were his speculations on the environmental demands of a species which determined where it might best flourish

---

[16] Smith, "The Early Forestry Movement in the United States," p. 328. A similar definition is given by the pioneer American Forester Gifford Pinchot in *Breaking New Ground* (New York, 1947), p. 1.

[17] For other comments on this period see Deevey, "A Re-examination of Thoreau's *Walden*," p. 8 f., and Kathryn Whitford, "Thoreau and the Woodlots of Concord," *New England Quarterly*, XXIII (September 1950), 294 ff.

[18] See for example XX, 258, 268, 280.

[19] See for example XX, 140, 152, 183, 255, 271, 280.

and what other species it might succeed. "It is an interesting inquiry," he wrote, to determine "which species shall grow on a given tract." Certainly the soil was involved, for massed red maples and swamp white oaks were quite common in wet places, lacking in uplands, but allowances must also be made for minute variations in the light and warmth available under different stands.[20] In these speculations, Thoreau arrived at the modern idea of the climax: that "in the natural state of things, when sufficient time is given, trees will be found occupying the places most suitable to each," so that the forest is generally "in a transition state to a settled and normal condition" (XX, 218).

Each of Thoreau's investigations of silvics—another that might be mentioned is his study of the rate of growth of various trees, especially pitch pines, to determine the most profitable age for cutting[21]—was adding to the foundation for a modern forest management and thus increasing the possibility of a union between satisfactory profits and the preservation of nature. However, for an understanding of the relation between Thoreau's forestry and his attitude to the economic order, the most significant point is perhaps that on the relative value of trees which originally sprouted from stumps and trees which originally sprang from seed.

When Timothy Dwight recognized that succession might be employed to make New England's forests "ever-living," he also described another method which his countrymen thought would achieve the same end. "When a field of wood is, in the language of our farmers, cut clean," wrote Dwight, that is, "when every tree is cut down, . . . vigorous shoots sprout from every stump, and having their nourishment supplied by the roots of the former tree, grow with a thrift and rapidity never seen in stems derived from the seeds. Good ground will thus yield a growth, amply sufficient for fuel, once in fourteen years."[22] In Thoreau's time as in Dwight's, it was chiefly this procedure, technically known as the coppice method, that was relied on to produce new woods around Concord.

Thoreau's investigation of the coppice method sprang from his

[20] XX, 134, 143, 258. See also XX, 147, 181.
[21] See for example XX, 175 f., 185 f., 190, 193 f., 197, 203–7, 232–39, 251.
[22] *Travels in New-England and New-York*, I, 80.

suspicion that it led to the destruction of an indispensable portion of nature. Shortly after he delivered his lecture on succession, he recorded his feeling that "the noblest trees and those which it took the longest to produce, and which are the longest-lived," such as chestnuts, oaks, and perhaps hickories, "are the first to become extinct under our present system and the hardest to reproduce" (XX, 135). Repeated clear-cutting and growth from sprouts was destroying "our noblest hardwood forests" (XX, 200) and replacing them "by pines and birches, of feebler growth than the primitive pines and birches, for want of a change of soil" (XX, 135).

This hypothesis Thoreau could test only with the rigor available to a natural historian, not with that of the scientific technician, but he applied himself to essentially the same problems singled out by his better-equipped successors.[23] He observed young shoots sprouted from stumps which had in turn sprouted from other stumps still outlined by their sides, and wished to know how long such regeneration could continue.[24] He speculated on whether old trunks would produce sprouts as readily as younger ones and whether sprouting was influenced by the season at which the tree was cut.[25] He thought that sprout trees would succumb to disease sooner than seedlings, being merely extensions of trunks and roots of a previous generation and thus old before their time.[26] He knew that sprouts grew more rapidly than seedlings, but suspected that their trunks were shaky, that with both trees and men "you must grow slowly to last long."[27]

Sickness prevented Thoreau from completing his studies; at the time he caught the cold which first became bronchitis and then became his death, he was still examining chestnut sprouts circled round the parent stump (XX, 290). But the direction of his investigations is clear to see: the coppice method might yield a quick turnover, but it did not produce the best trees; fuel perhaps, but not wide boards and

---

[23] Ralph C. Hawley, *The Practice of Silviculture* (5th ed.; New York, 1946), pp. 176–87.

[24] XX, 93 f., 105, 168 f., 223, 256, 268 f.

[25] XX, 157, 165, 169, 177, 211, 212 f., 276 f.

[26] XX, 145, 190 f.

[27] XX, 191. See also XX, 217.

noble symbols of heroism and aspiration.[28] To grow these one must start from seed, and the seed of oak and chestnut grew best under other trees.

The groves of chestnut which once enriched the Concord landscape had been eaten up in railroad sleepers, planks, and wooden rails, and there was danger in Thoreau's day that the species would become extinct.[29] Farmers complained that they could find no seedlings to transplant. But in his exploration of the undergrowth beneath other species Thoreau found many young chestnuts, probably planted by squirrels. They were especially plentiful under pines.[30] It followed then that they might be allowed to grow under the shelter of other trees until strong enough to withstand transplanting. Moreover, they might even succeed to the covering species if the latter were properly removed. "Thus it appears," concluded Thoreau, "that by a judicious letting Nature alone merely we might recover our chestnut wood in the course of a century" (XX, 138).

In a similar way the township might recover its old oak wood. Thoreau did not find beneath the older trees many young oaks ready to shoot up if given space and sunlight but noticed them in great numbers under pines.[31] In the vicinity of Concord, he concluded, "the pine woods are a natural nursery of oaks" (XX, 139), establishing themselves on unoccupied or exhausted lands and preparing the soil for their more demanding successors (XX, 130, 150). But the seedling oaks flourished beneath the dense pines only from six to ten years. After that they needed a wider prospect and might be transplanted to open ground or favored by first cutting branches off the pines and at the proper time felling the cover altogether to leave the oaks in control of the plot (XX, 139 f.). The owner who planned to cut a fine oak wood and wished his descendants to enjoy its equal "should be con-

---

[28] Recent forestry is in essential agreement; see Whitford, "Thoreau and the Woodlots of Concord," p. 304 f., and Hawley, *The Practice of Silviculture*, p. 184 f.

[29] Thoreau was thinking of its extinction by man; it has since been made scarce by the chestnut blight.

[30] XX, 137 f., 188 f.

[31] XX, 139 f., 144 f., 150, 180–83, 249 f.

sidering how to favor the growth of pines" (XX, 213), to which the new oaks would succeed in their turn.

Whatever the inadequacies of Thoreau's pioneering approximation of forest realities in Massachusetts,[32] his underlying principle was a sound one. He came back always to succession, the natural laws whose operation led the forest by stages toward the climax. Only by taking advantage of these could man grow trees to serve both lower ends and higher.

But the owners of Concord wood lots were for the most part ignorant of natural laws, shallow empirical men who could better see the immediate dollar than the many that might be scientifically planned for. Thoreau was disgusted by their improvident practices in the woodland. A foresighted husbandman, he held, examines the ground beneath his trees to "ascertain what kind of wood is about to take the place of the old and how abundantly, in order that he may act understandingly and determine if it is best to clear the land or not" (XX, 94). But again and again he discovered his neighbors ignoring nature's preparations for a new crop and violating the forest's laws to their own ultimate disadvantage. The most common malpractice involved the cutting or burning of seedling trees left on newly cut land.

Sometimes a farmer who used his plow or bushwhack on the young pines annually invading his field finally decided to give up and allow nature to present him with a wood lot. One such owner, writes Thoreau, "blind to his own interests," plowed the little trees under "and got a few beans for his pains," but the pines "grew while he slept" and were "so thick and promising" that he at length "concluded not to cut his own fingers any more, *i.e.*, not further than up to the last joint," and allowed the trees to form a border to his planting. But "they would have covered the half or perhaps the whole of his barren field before this, if he had let them" (XX, 128).

Other farmers refused to give in. One, felling his pines but unable to see beyond grass, repeatedly cut down the hickories which had

---

[32] Deevey, for example, suggests that he "overemphasized the reversibility of plant succession" ("A Re-examination of Thoreau's *Walden*," p. 8).

succeeded them and got, in a few years, not a valuable young wood lot but a sterile field on which the succession cycle would have to begin anew with birches and other first growth (XX, 94). A second, cutting dense pine, burned over the land, killed the many seedling oaks that had been nursed in the grove, and planted rye, a procedure which could yield only "starved pasture" in the end. "What a fool!" exclaimed Thoreau on seeing what he had done. "He has got his dollars for the pine timber, and now he wishes to get his bushels of grain and finger the dollars that they will bring; and then, Nature, you may have your way again. Let us purchase a mass for his soul. A greediness that defeats its own ends" (XX, 131 f.).[33]

But what was to be done to bring such men's actions into correspondence with the laws of nature? The answer toward which Thoreau took a first step in the fall of 1860 is a commonplace of our day, but it is not usually associated with the author of "Civil Disobedience." Commenting on the last-mentioned farmer, who had ruined his one chance of getting oaks in order to profit from a little rye, Thoreau wrote: "I am chagrined for him. That he should call himself an agriculturalist! He needs to have a guardian placed over him. A forest-warden should be appointed by the town. Overseers of poor husbandmen" (XX, 131). Convinced that the individual involved was unable to see beyond the sale of his next harvest to a source of profit that would also give the whole community a grove of trees serving higher ends than money, Thoreau was willing to restrict the area reserved for the action of the man's private conscience.

Thoreau's conclusion was inevitable from his premises. When he accepted a profit-directed economy as impersonally dictated necessity he did not cease to insist that acquisition should be subordinated to the higher end of self-culture. Morality—to use the word broadly—had always been more important to him than possessions, and it continued to be so. Within the narrow limits of forest management he experimented, as he had done at the pond, in the relation between

---

[33] Other examples of mismanagement will be found in XX, 126–28, 132 f., 145 f., 150 f., 176 f., 187 f., 198. An example of proper management is described in XX, 191 f., where Thoreau shows how a farmer took advantage of white pine and pitch pine succession relations to produce "a valuable and salable woodland."

the order of production and the higher order of morality, attempting once again to discover how the two might be made congruent. But his beginnings of a solution within this narrow field necessarily came into conflict with minds educated to venality, and he was forced, like others both before him and after, to advocate control of the material acquisition of the individual in favor of the spiritual appropriation of the many. To achieve this control, Thoreau turned to the instrument of the many nearest to hand and most proportionate to the task: the peaceful processes of government. In another aspect of this general problem, Negro slavery, the peaceful instruments of the majority would in his opinion prove inadequate, and Thoreau would become a supporter of a government at war.

III

The conflict between the material acquisition of the one and the spiritual appropriation of the many is the key to Thoreau's advocacy of conservation, which complements his research in forestry and carries his social thought to government ownership.

A little more than four years before he built his hut on Emerson's lake frontage at Walden, Thoreau had attempted to rent or buy some farmland on which to declare his independence. When he failed from poverty he fell back defiantly on the contention that the spiritual farming which really interested him could be carried on without occupancy. "What have I to do with plows?" he asked. "I cut another furrow than you see" (VII, 245).

Looking back on this or a similar experience in the summer of 1851, he was still able to say to himself that though he had failed to buy a certain plot "for want of money," he had harvested there annually nonetheless—"in my own fashion" (VIII, 439). But the previous winter he had already recognized that the end of such free spiritual appropriation of nature was coming into sight. "I trust," he had written, "that the walkers of the present day are conscious of the blessings which they enjoy in the comparative freedom with which they can ramble over the country . . . , anticipating with compassion that future day when possibly it will be partitioned off into so-called pleasure-grounds, where only a few may enjoy the narrow and exclusive pleasure which is compatible with ownership,—when walking over the surface of God's earth shall be construed to mean trespassing on some gentleman's grounds, when fences shall be multiplied and man traps and other engines invented to confine men to the public road" (VIII, 156 f.).

For Thoreau and his frequent companion Channing the "evil days" (V, 216) of that suburbanized future had already begun to arrive, and the lengthening, branching fences diverted their walks toward the pine barrens, swamps, and streams. "The river is my own highway," wrote Thoreau in the spring of 1852, "the only wild and unfenced part of the world hereabouts" (X, 77). Ten months later he repeated the statement with a significant addition: "In relation to the river, I find my natural rights least infringed on. It is an extensive 'common' still left. Certain savage liberties still prevail in the oldest and most civilized countries" (XI, 45 f.).

Access to nature was thus an inherent right of mankind which had been respected, he believed, in more primitive societies but was being progressively eroded by civilization. "Among the Indians," he wrote in a late manuscript, "the earth & its productions generally were common & free to all the tribe, like the air & water—but among us who have supplanted the Indians, the public retain only a small yard or common in the middle of the village, with perhaps a grave-yard beside it, & the right of way, by sufferance, by a particular narrow route, which is annually becoming narrower, from one such yard to another." He was "not overflowing with respect and gratitude" to the men who had thus laid out New England's villages, "for I think," he declared, "that a 'prentice hand liberated from Old English prejudices could have done much better in this new world. If they were in earnest seeking thus far away 'freedom to worship God,' as some assure us—why did they not secure a little more of it, when it was so cheap? At the same time that they built meeting-houses why did they not preserve from desecration & destruction far grander temples not made with hands?"[34]

---

[34] From "Portion of Holograph Journal, 1860–1861," now in the Henry W. and Albert A. Berg Collection of the New York Public Library, by whose permission it is here quoted.

To make up for the failure of the original settlers, Thoreau advocated conservation. The "natural features which make a township
handsome" should be preserved for the public and not surrendered to
individuals: "a river, with its waterfalls and meadows, a lake, a hill,
a cliff or individual rocks, a forest, and ancient trees standing singly"—as many as possible of the "precious natural objects of rare
beauty" (XX, 304 f.). This radical principle of conservation Thoreau
applied concretely in three distinct areas: original wilderness un-
changed by man, humanized nature shaped by its role in the economy, and wholly domesticated nature along streets and roads.

The rationale behind Thoreau's desire to preserve samples of wilderness parallels the extended metaphor in "Walking." Primitive
nature unmodified by man is needed as "a resource and background,
the raw material of all our civilization." The poet, for example, both
for "strength" and for "beauty," must periodically "travel the logger's
path and the Indian's trail, to drink at some new and more bracing
fountain of the Muses, far in the recesses of the wilderness" (III,
172 f.).

Thoreau found the closest approach to original nature in Maine,
and he concluded the account of his second trip to that territory with
a request for "national preserves," presumably owned by the federal
government but how acquired he does not say, "in which the bear and
panther, and some even of the hunter race, may still exist, and not be
'civilized off the face of the earth'" (III, 173).[35] Similarly, the last
pages of his journal include a statement that the top of New Hampshire's Mt. Washington, then in dispute between two individuals,
"should not be private property" at all but be left "unappropriated,"
together with its approaches, so that access to its inspirations would
not depend on the generosity of private owners (XX, 305).

The wild, however, was not the poet's true home but only its essential supplement. It was humanized nature that provided the only
adequate natural environment for civilized man. Thoreau first real-

---

[35] It is chiefly these words which lead Paul H. Oehser ("Pioneers in
Conservation: Footnote to the History of an Idea," *Nature Magazine,*
XXXVIII [April 1945], 189) to consider Thoreau as "perhaps . . . Amer-
ica's first real conservationist."

ized this fact (as was pointed out earlier in these pages) on his trip
to Mount Katahdin in the summer of 1846. He stated it most explicitly, however, in "Chesuncook," published in 1858 but recounting
the experiences of his trip to Maine five years earlier.

Despite the impulse whose satisfaction demanded the wilderness,
Thoreau found it "a relief" to get back from Maine to the "smooth
but still varied landscape" around Concord, for it was this, and not
primitive nature, that a civilized man needed for his "permanent resi-
dence." Placed in the original forest, such a man must eventually
pine, "like a cultivated plant which clasps its fibres about a crude and
undissolved mass of peat." He needed the frontier farmers and the
lumbermen to tame the wilderness and prepare a nature on which
civilization could sustain itself. Poets in particular, such at least as
"compose the mass of any literature," though they needed breaths of
a stronger air, were inspired chiefly by "the partially cultivated country" rather than by the wild and could not thrive unless the "logger
and pioneer" had first "humanized Nature" for them.

But nature was not to be subdued too far, not to the point of
"elaborately and willfully wealth-constructed parks and gardens."
Perhaps, thought Thoreau, it was such fields and woods as lay about
Concord, "with the primitive swamps scattered here and there in their
midst, but not prevailing over them," that were "the perfection of
parks and groves, gardens, arbors, paths, vistas, and landscapes"—"the
common which each village possesses, its true paradise" (III, 171 f.).
"Each town," he wrote the year after the publication of "Chesuncook," "should have a park, or rather a primitive forest, of five hundred or a thousand acres, where a stick should never be cut for fuel,
a common possession forever, for instruction and recreation" (XVIII,
387).

Had the original settlers of Concord been sufficiently foresighted,
thought Thoreau, they might easily have reserved such a "true paradise" for the townspeople. "All Walden Wood," he wrote in 1859,
"might have been preserved for our park forever, with Walden in
its midst, and the Easterbrooks Country, an unoccupied area of some
four square miles, might have been our huckleberry-field" (XVIII,
387). The town's first planners, he added in the late manuscript
quoted from earlier, should also have "made the river available as a

common possession forever. The town collectively should at least have done as much as an individual of taste who owns an equal area commonly does in England. Indeed," he continued, "not only the channel, but one or both banks of every river should be a public highway—for a river is not useful merely to float on. In this case, one bank might have been reserved as a public walk & the trees that adorned it have been protected, and frequent avenues have been provided leading to it from the main street."

But though the conservation of parks, rivers, and river banks was the responsibility of "the town collectively," Thoreau did not rely on the power of local government to regain the lands which had been surrendered to private ownership. Instead, reducing one tradition of American agrarianism to philanthropy, he fell back on inheritance. After the 1859 journal passage on Walden Wood and the Easterbrooks Country, he went on to say: "If any owners of these tracts are about to leave the world without natural heirs who need or deserve to be specially remembered, they will do wisely to abandon their possession to all, and not will them to some individual who perhaps has enough already" (XVIII, 387).

Elsewhere, however, Thoreau does speak of a "committee appointed to see that the beauty of the town received no detriment" (XX, 304), and when he incorporates this statement into the late manuscript we have quoted from he seems to be thinking of some governmental privilege such as eminent domain. Before it he writes that he does not consider a man "fit to be the founder of a state or even of a town" who does not preserve its best natural features for public use, and immediately after it: "If here is the largest boulder in the country, then it should not belong to an individual nor be made into doorsteps." Action by the local government to appropriate boulders, river banks, hilltops, seems to be a natural extension of its other activities. "There are a few hopeful signs," writes Thoreau in the manuscript. "There is the growing library—& then the town does set trees along the highway—but does not the broad landscape itself deserve attention?"

The action of the selectmen in having trees set along the highway was praised by Thoreau more than once, both in his journal and in his lecture "Autumnal Tints." Within towns and between towns he wanted mankind to move beneath branches. "Let us have a good many maples and hickories and scarlet oaks," he demanded. "A village is not complete, unless it have these trees to mark the season in it" (V, 276). When he entered Massachusetts after an excursion to New Hampshire in 1858, he was happy to get away from the "long bleak or sunny roads" of the Granite State and take advantage of the shade trees planted by the older Bay State. But he was still not satisfied. A farmer apparently ran over when he made a fire by the roadside. "What barbarians we are!" he exclaimed to himself. "The convenience of the traveller is very little consulted. He merely has the privilege of crossing somebody's farm by a particular narrow and maybe unpleasant path." The sides of a road, like the banks of a river, "should belong to mankind inalienably." The road itself "should be of ample width and adorned with trees expressly for the use of the traveller," and "there should be broad recesses in it, especially at springs and watering-places, where he can turn out and rest, or camp if he will" (XVII, 55).

IV

The forest conservationists of Thoreau's generation did not yet think, as Thoreau already did, of a union between satisfactory profits and the preservation of nature. Their argument did not include the money to be made from trees but was based chiefly on the salutary indirect influences of trees on the economy.[36] "Whenever half a dozen people got together in those days to talk about forestry," wrote Gifford Pinchot of a time even later in the century, "they discoursed on the effects of forests upon climate, streamflow, and rainfall. But the idea of a continuous succession of forest crops was outside the field of practical politics."[37]

The best known statement on the subject of forest influences produced by Thoreau's generation is in George Perkins Marsh's *Man*

---

[36] Frederick A. Ogg, *National Progress, 1907–1917*, Vol. 27 of *The American Nation: A History* (New York and London, 1918), p. 97 f. Gifford Pinchot, "How Conservation Began in the United States," *Agricultural History*, XI (October 1937), 257 f.

[37] "How Conservation Began in the United States," p. 258.

and Nature, first published in 1864.[38] Marsh argued that the American people could not attain their much-desired material improvements unless they first restored some part of the equilibrium of nature that was being excessively disturbed by their economy.

Nature, he maintained, is essentially stable. If it were not for man's interference, the proportions of land and water, of precipitation and evaporation, of heat and cold, as well as the distribution of plants and animals, would be "maintained by natural compensations in a state of approximate equilibrium" (p. 31), changing only with the slow influence of geological evolution. The earth in this stable natural condition is not, however, "completely adapted to the use of man, but only to the sustenance of wild animals and wild vegetation" (p. 36). Man, as well as the portions of nature which enter into his economy, cannot exist and develop without to a certain degree disturbing the equilibrium. But this degree he has unfortunately exceeded, and in doing so has let loose upon himself the "destructive energies" (p. 43) normally checked by the forces he has tampered with. Proportion has been succeeded by excess — deluges and droughts, swamps and dry barrens—and the economy has suffered. It is therefore essential to restore the equilibrium wherever it has been excessively disturbed and to prevent its excessive disturbance wherever new lands are being occupied.

In his long chapter on forests (pp. 148–397), Marsh presented a detailed and documented account of the value of woods in preserving the balance of nature and of the disastrous excess following upon their destruction. Keep the woods, he argued, and the land will be sheltered from parching winds, the soil protected from unusual heat and cold, and the temperature of the air range less widely from its mean. Lose

---

[38] A brief history of the subject of forest influences in the United States and elsewhere is in Joseph Kittredge, *Forest Influences: the Effects of Woody Vegetation on Climate, Water, and Soil, with Applications to the Conservation of Water and the Control of Floods and Erosion* (New York, Toronto, and London, 1948), pp. 6–15. The copy of Marsh cited in this study is not of the first but of a later edition: *The Earth as Modified by Human Action: A New Edition of Man and Nature* (New York, 1882); however, the text proper, as distinct from footnotes and appendixes, is not substantially different from that of the first.

them and tempests will sweep over the land to suck out its moisture, the climate will run to extremes, and the soil will be "alternately parched by the fervors of summer and seared by the rigors of winter" (p. 301). Preserve the forests and they will help distribute precipitation equally over the seasons and over the land and will regulate the absorption of water and the flow of streams and rivers. Destroy them and rain and snow will descend irregularly, the soil will be unable to store large volumes of water, and nothing will prevent "the sudden rise of rivers, the violence of floods, the formation of destructive torrents, and the abrasion of the surface by the action of running water" (p. 300).

Marsh's picture of a deforested world contained more than a hint of the bogeyman. He felled the barriers against his rhetoric and it swept over the page to create a globe whose rivers had become unnavigable, whose harbors were shoaled by sand bars, and whose land was eroded and barren. His essential point, however, was well taken, and recent generations have witnessed forest conservation, tree planting, and dam building that are in no slight degree the fruit of the writers of whom Marsh is representative.

Thoreau, too, was much concerned with forest influences, with the influences of all of nature on mankind. His ultimate concern, however, was not with the effect of nature on the human economy but on the human spirit. An example of this distinction is his comment in "Autumnal Tints" on the circulation of the elements.

The conservationist argument which Thoreau uses was thus summed up by a contemporary: "The roots of the trees, penetrating to a considerable depth, draw up from the subsoil certain nutritive salts that enter into the substance of all parts of the tree. This is restored to the surface by every tree or branch that falls and moulders upon it, and the leaves increase its bulk still more by their annual decay."[39] Presenting this thesis in the section on "Fallen Leaves," Thoreau first limits himself to transforming its vehicle. "The trees," he writes, "are now repaying the earth with interest what they have taken from it. They are discounting. They are about to add a leaf's

---

[39] Wilson Flagg, *The Woods and By-Ways of New England* (Boston, 1872), p. 236 f.

thickness to the depth of the soil." Their decay "prepares the virgin mould for future corn-fields and forests, on which the earth fattens."

But he is not content with having raised the form to a higher level. In the next paragraph he begins to transform the thesis itself. The fallen leaves "live in the soil, whose fertility and bulk they increase, and in the forests that spring from it. They stoop to rise, to mount higher in coming years, by subtle chemistry, climbing by the sap in the trees; and the sapling's first fruits thus shed, transmuted at last, may adorn its crown, when, in after years, it has become the monarch of the forest." The circulation of the elements has now become a trope by which Thoreau communicates the transcendentalist faith in the ascending spiral within each man and the universe.

But this in turn suggests still another analogy, and Thoreau writes: "They that soared so loftily, how contentedly they return to dust again, and are laid low, resigned to lie and decay at the foot of the tree, and afford nourishment to new generations of their kind, as well as to flutter on high! They teach us how to die. One wonders if the time will ever come when men, with their boasted faith in immortality, will lie down as gracefully and as ripe,—with such an Indian-summer serenity will shed their bodies, as they do their hair and nails" (V, 268–70).

Upon a foundation of the influence of forests in maintaining the balance of nature, Thoreau has thus raised a superstructure fusing his teachings on self-culture, progress, and religion. He does not discard the economic value of nature, but he transforms it, as he did in his silviculture, to serve an additional and higher end.

Thoreau was not, of course, the only conservationist whose motive included what Marsh called "poetical" rather than "economical" views of the subject (p. 327). Such views formed part of the argument of the Bostonians and New Yorkers who in Thoreau's time and later advocated parks as a necessary complement to the massed buildings and hidden earth of their cities.[40]

---

[40] A short and inadequate account is Charles E. Doell and Gerald B. Fitzgerald, *A Brief History of Parks and Recreation in the United States* (Chicago, 1954). Materials on the park movement in Boston will be found in Ellen Wright, *Elizur Wright's Appeals for the Middlesex Fells and the Forests, with a Sketch of What he Did for Both* (Medford, Massachusetts, 1904).

Among the most articulate of these people was Andrew Jackson Downing, the architect of moneyed suburbanism, who designed "rural cottages" and "cottage villas" hedged and laned by a genteel, premeditated nature. In the preface, dated 1842, to a collection of such designs, Downing explained to his potential employers the rationale behind his insistence that a country house be surrounded by an appropriate landscape. He wished to awaken in his readers, he said, a sense of "the grace, the elegance, or the picturesqueness of fine forms" that could be produced in house and grounds, "a sense which will not only refine and elevate the mind, but open to it new and infinite sources of delight." Moreover, he continued, "so closely are the Beautiful and the True allied, that we shall find, if we become sincere lovers of the grace, the harmony, and the loveliness with which rural homes and rural life are capable of being invested, that we are silently opening our hearts to an influence which is higher and deeper than the mere *symbol*; and that if we thus worship in the true spirit, we shall attain a nearer view of the Great Master, whose words, in all his material universe, are written in lines of Beauty."[41]

In 1846 Downing became editor of *The Horticulturist and Journal of Rural Art and Taste,* and in this magazine he extended his argument on behalf of nature to roadsides and parks.

In an editorial of 1849 he urged the necessity of having the streets of small towns planted with trees. At the very least, he wrote, they would "cast a grateful veil over the deformity of a country home." But then he went beyond his livelihood and argued that the trees would not only provide shade and serve as firebreaks but would exercise a salutary influence on the character of the townspeople. A village with treeless streets, he declared, "ought to be looked upon as in a condition not less pitiable than a community without a schoolmaster, or a teacher of religion," while one "adorned by its avenues of elms, and made tasteful by the affection of its inhabitants" is a place "where order, good character, and virtuous deportment most of all adorn the lives and daily conduct of its people."[42]

---

[41] *Cottage Residences; or, A Series of Designs for Rural Cottages and Cottage Villas, and their Gardens and Grounds, Adapted to North America* (4th ed.; New York, 1853), pp. vi–vii.

[42] *Horticulturist*, III (June 1849), 546 f.

From roadsides Downing progressed, by a somber but understandable route, to city parks. Both Boston and Philadelphia had established rural cemeteries, Mount Auburn and Laurel Hill, and Downing noted that in nine months of 1848 the latter had been visited by thirty thousand people. Did not this interest in rural cemeteries, he asked, "prove that public gardens, established in a liberal and suitable manner, near our large cities, would be equally successful?"[43]

His first suggestion was a privately financed company which would buy a site in the suburbs of a large city and develop it into what would today be called a botanical garden. Those who owned shares would use the park without charge; the public in general would pay a fee. The collection of labeled plants, which might be made the subject of lectures, would be obviously educational, and to them might be added band concerts. There would be walks for those who admired landscape, and refreshments for the weary. The project, he believed, would not only pay its way but "foster the love of rural beauty" and "largely civilize and refine the national character."[44]

In 1850, Downing took the step from private to public ownership. Each new American town, he suggested, should be laid out around a central park which would always be held "as joint property, and for the common use of the whole village."[45] It was a natural development of this suggestion that he should become an advocate of the Central Park for New York which had earlier been thought of by William Cullen Bryant.[46] Downing's conception of this park was a combination of his original botanical garden and ideas which he had gathered in 1850 on a tour of the parks in and about London. It was not only to provide relaxation and amusement or to supplement the schools with its concerts, its exhibitions, its labeled plants, and its collections of animals. Above all these—and it is this which concerns us here—the park was to exercise an elevating moral influence on all who frequented it.[47]

---

[43] *Horticulturist,* IV (July 1849), 10–11.

[44] *Horticulturist,* IV (July 1849), 12.

[45] *Horticulturist,* IV (June 1850), 540.

[46] Allan Nevins, *The Evening Post: A Century of Journalism* (New York, 1922), p. 193.

[47] *Horticulturist,* VI (August 1851), 345–49.

There are passages in the later writings of Henry Thoreau which resemble statements by Downing and may suggest that to some degree Thoreau's conception of the spiritual uses of nature began to accommodate itself to the genteel tradition.

Like Downing, for example, Thoreau attached an exaggerated and sentimental importance to tree-lined streets as evidence of the mental and moral state of the people who lived on them. "Show me two villages," he wrote in "Autumnal Tints," "one embowered in trees and blazing with all the glories of October, the other a merely trivial and treeless waste, or with only a single tree or two for suicides, and I shall be sure that in the latter will be found the most starved and bigoted religionists and the most desperate drinkers" (V, 277). Occasionally he too took the elms for a symbol of ideal village domesticity. Their presence, he wrote in a journal entry of 1851, shows "a nobler husbandry than the raising of corn and potatoes" (VIII, 281). And six years later it seemed to him that every distant elm was "the vignette to an unseen idyllic poem," and he fancied that he could hear "the house-dog's bark and lowing of the cows seeking admittance to their yard," and that he could see "the master and mistress and the hired man" sitting down at the tea table "in their shirt-sleeves" (XVI, 89).

Equally with Downing, Thoreau believed that a true nearness to nature would bring a man closer to deity, and at times, as when he wrote that to keep glimpsing heaven he must make his life "more moral, more pure and innocent" (XI, 517), he introduced into this abstraction his own troubles with the physical and prepared a formula that might well have served gentility in its appeal to youths and women.

But both Thoreau and Downing made nature an ally in the conflicts of society, and the essential disagreement between the two men on these larger issues imparted wholly different directions to their common belief that whatever is beyond the economic and biological in nature should be made available to the people by means of public parks.

For Downing there was a fixed ideal—the gentleman—identified with the self-interest of a growing leisure class. The "point of departure of his philosophy," wrote his friend George William Curtis, was the home; he wished "that the landscape should be lovely, and the houses graceful and beautiful, and the fruit fine, and the flowers perfect" only because "these were all dependencies and ornaments of home, and home was the sanctuary of the highest human affections." But the home was that of the rich gentleman. "The workman, the author, the artist were entirely subjugated in him to the gentleman," writes Curtis. "That was his favorite idea."[48] And a more recent writer adds that Downing and his pupils so far catered to genteel idleness that they "urged keeping the entire machinery of an estate out of sight so that flowers might bloom, lawns be mowed, walks swept, 'by invisible hands,' at night or 'at such hours as the family is not supposed to come out.' "[49]

In an editorial on Central Park, Downing took the wealthy to task for not understanding "the elevating influences of the beautiful in nature and art, when enjoyed in common" by all classes of society. In the parks of Europe, he wrote, rich and poor "enjoy together the same music, breathe the same atmosphere of art, enjoy the same scenery, and grow into social freedom by the very influence of easy intercourse, space and beauty, that surround them." Similiarly in America, he hoped, public parks would serve the cause of social stability. "The higher social and artistic elements of every man's nature lie dormant within him," he asserted, "and every laborer is a possible gentleman, not by the possession of money or fine clothes—but through the refining influence of intellectual and moral culture."[50]

For Thoreau there was an evolutionary and therefore indeterminate ideal—self-culture—to which no group in his America appeared to be committed. Earlier pages of this study attempted to demonstrate that in one aspect of his relation to spiritual nature after the return from the pond Thoreau sought in vain for absolute principles, unavailable to him within the social order, upon which to found a new life dedicated to this ripening of the self. Concurrent with this search was the uneven growth of his philosophy of social reform, and it was

---

[48] "Memoir" of Andrew Jackson Downing, first published in 1853 and reprinted as an appendix to the tenth edition of Downing's *Landscape Gardening* (New York, 1921), pp. 407, 409 f.

[49] Carl Carmer, *The Hudson* (New York and Toronto, 1939), p. 241.

[50] *Horticulturist,* VI (August 1851), 348 f.

with this philosophy that Thoreau was integrating his attitude toward the spiritual in nature in the second and more significant aspect of its development.

The chief mechanism of this attachment was the conscious projection of correspondences already illustrated in Thoreau's metaphor of the circulation of the elements. Whatever in nature was beyond the economic and biological (save deity itself) lost all objectivity, and man could view it the way the poet saw the pines in Maine, "as his own shadow in the air" (III, 135), drawing upon nature for the "raw material of tropes and symbols with which to describe his life" (XI, 135). It was a humanizing of the spiritual aspect of nature by man's mind corresponding to the humanizing of its biological aspect by his economy.

In projecting his social philosophy into nature, Thoreau tried first of all to liberate his audience from the low principle of acquisition and to turn their minds to the higher goal of self-culture. Obsessed as he had long been with the analogy between the life of man and the seasons of the year, he turned in his own maturity to the image of ripeness and in paragraphs free of the stridency of his youth guided his hearers to the conclusion that they too must grow toward a ripeness and must mature their own harvest.

In "Wild Apples," for example, he tells at length of "little thickets of apple trees" which spring up in pastures and are browsed on and kept down by the cattle but defend themselves by growing along the ground in "pyramidal, stiff, twiggy" masses and spreading each year "until at last they are so broad that they become their own fence, when some interior shoot, which their foes cannot reach, darts upward with joy; for it has not forgotten its high calling, and bears its own peculiar fruit in triumph." The image speaks for itself, but Thoreau is intent enough on results to point the moral. "What a lesson to man!" he exclaims. "So are human beings, referred to the highest standard, the celestial fruit which they suggest and aspire to bear, browsed on by fate; and only the most persistent and strongest genius defends itself and prevails, sends a tender scion upward at last, and drops its perfect fruit on the ungrateful earth" (V, 303–7).

In "Autumnal Tints" the vehicle of his correspondence is color, yellows in part, but chiefly reds: the "purplish mist" of the grasses, the "deep, brilliant purple" and "lake red" of the poke, the crimsoned maples standing like "burning bushes" in the meadows, the "intense, burning" hue of the leaves of scarlet oak which at a distance make their trees "unanimously red." He writes as if to incite the reader to an intoxication, even a sensuality. The sepals of the poke "are a brilliant lake red, with crimson flame-like reflections"—"all on fire with ripeness." The plant "speaks to our blood" (V, 254). In the journal he had said, "Nature here is full of blood and heat and luxuriance" (VIII, 490). But object and emotion were to fuse in the metaphor and endow the idea itself with their own energy. The poke is "the emblem of a successful life concluded by a death not premature, which is an ornament to Nature. What if we were to mature as perfectly, root and branch, glowing in the midst of our decay, like the poke! I confess that it excites me to behold them. I cut one for a cane, for I would fain handle and lean on it. I love to press the berries between my fingers, and see their juice staining my hand" (V, 254 f.).

Limiting himself to the leaves of trees and wild grasses, which serve no use on plates or in market stalls, Thoreau sharpened the analogy. He had learned from some physiologist that as leaves approach fall they breathe more oxygen, and he founded on this supposition a freedom from the earth and an increasing attachment to sun and air, a soaring from the lower to the higher. Writing of the scarlet oak, whose leaves have so little flatness as to be "only a few sharp points extending from a midrib," Thoreau again fuses his morality with a realized object: "The leaves of very young plants are, like those of full-grown oaks of other species, more entire, simple, and lumpish in their outlines, but these, raised high on old trees, have solved the leafy problem. Lifted higher and higher, and sublimated more and more, putting off some earthiness and cultivating more intimacy with the light each year, they have at length the least possible amount of earthy matter, and the greatest spread and grasp of skyey influence" (V, 278).

Parallel with liberation from the body is liberation from venality. The finest purple grass flourishes "at the base of dry hills, just above the edge of the meadows, where the greedy mower does not deign to whet his scyth; for this is a thin and poor grass, beneath his notice." But perhaps "because it is so beautiful he does not know that it exists;

for the same eye does not see this and timothy" (V, 253). Writing of the autumn elms, Thoreau desires to accept them, as in the journal entry quoted earlier, for evidence of higher aims. "Under these bright rustling yellow piles just ready to fall on the heads of the walkers, how can any crudity or greenness of thought or act prevail?" He is tempted to go among these trees "as to a husking of thoughts, now dry and ripe, and ready to be separated from their integuments"— "but, alas!" he confesses, "I foresee that it will be chiefly husks and little thought, blasted pig-corn, fit only for cob-meal,—for, as you sow, so shall you reap" (V, 263 f.). No man can soar while tied to the table and the cash box.

Both "Wild Apples" and "Autumnal Tints" are, properly speaking, polemics, disputing at varying levels of intensity with the values indoctrinated by acquisitive society. And like all polemics, they exaggerate and require the mediation of context. In a journal entry of 1851 Thoreau expresses the wish that "we might make more use of leaves than we do," perhaps to fill mattresses or for fodder or litter (IX, 63). A few days earlier, seeing birch sprouts turned into hoops for casks, he had written, "I am pleased to learn that a man has detected any *use* in wood or stone or any material, or, in other words, its relation to man" (IX, 36). In the end there were always the coupled opposites, relation to spirit and relation to the body and economy on which spirit rested, and always the problem of their reconciliation. It is in the insistence on the modification of the lower to keep making possible the continually evolving higher that Thoreau differs essentially from Downing. To see the primacy of this insistence and its effect on his social thought, we must return again to Thoreau's advocacy of conservation.

V

Thoreau's demand for public conservation, whether of wilderness tracts, large parks, or rows of trees, can be adequately explained by the two concepts already referred to: man's need for both wild and humanized nature, and the tendency of private owners to exclude other people from their lands. But his rationale included a third element incompletely integrated with the others and perhaps more significant.

Its starting point is the tendency of private owners not only to fence mankind off from nature but actually to destroy nature. In Concord (as we have already seen) Thoreau witnessed the destruction of humanized nature by men who cut their wood lots without providing for the succession of a new stand. In Maine he encountered a similar shortsighted destruction of the wild forest.

On his trip to Mount Katahdin, made during the Walden experiment and dominated (as has been shown) by its ideology, Thoreau was not yet ready to be self-consciously aware of the need for conservation. But he gathered ample evidence preparing the way for the later conclusion. Though he himself gave instructions for cutting and burning timber in order to prepare land for cultivation (III, 15), he was distressed by the sight of a hundred acres newly felled and still smoking and by its implication: "the whole of that solid and interminable forest . . . doomed to be gradually devoured thus by fire, like shavings, and no man be warmed by it" (III, 18 f.). He also saw much of lumbering on this trip, noticed the fire-breeding carelessness with which the lumberers treated the forest after the best white pine had been taken out (III, 45), and concluded that the ambition of mankind in Maine seemed to be "to drive the forest all out of the country, from every solitary beaver swamp and mountain-side, as soon as possible" (III, 5 f.).

Thoreau's trip to Chesuncook Lake in 1853 provided additional evidence of this destructivity. But when he came to write it up—the account was not published, as has been noted, until 1858—he was ready to contrast the motive which led to the ravaging of the forest with another which led to its preservation.

Talking shop with the lumbermen, watching his companions kill a moose, Thoreau learned "how base or coarse are the motives which commonly carry men into the wilderness." Neither lumberman nor professional hunter was anything more than mercenary. The first tried to find cuttable timber—as much as he could possibly get out; the second tried to kill moose—as many as he could possibly skin. But "there is a higher law affecting our relation to pines as well as to men," declared Thoreau. Pine boards and moose hides have their "petty and accidental" functions, "for everything may serve a lower as well as a higher use." But the living pine "is no more lumber than man is, and to be made into boards and houses is no more its true and highest use than the truest use of a man is to be cut down and made into manure." It is not the man who performs economic functions upon the pines—cuts them, planes them, or distills their turpentine—who makes the "truest use" of them but rather the poet, "who loves them as his own shadow in the air, and lets them stand." "It is the living spirit of the tree," wrote Thoreau, "not its spirit of turpentine, with which I sympathize and which heals my cuts" (III, 133–35).

This exposition of the two opposing categories in their abstract and artistically polarized forms, like the similar one in his two late lectures, should not be mistaken for the totality of Thoreau's opinion. He did not mean to starve the community's body while feeding its soul. It has already been pointed out that the nature which he considered to be man's proper environment was not the wilderness but humanized nature, in which lumbermen, hunters, and frontier farmers had already been active. The properly managed wood lots which his silviculture made possible were not untouchable sacred groves but large stands which continued to provide lumber without ever being wholly cut down. Humanized nature might feed man's economy without starving his soul. Activities aimed solely at profit, however, served nothing but the economy. The sinfulness of the lumberman and professional hunter did not lie either in changing trees into boards or moose into hides but in that search for money which led them to cut and kill without rule whenever they could do so.

In the last years of his short life, Thoreau came to believe that the destruction of nature and the primacy of the material motive were in his own time inextricably bound up with private property, and opposition to the latter became an element in the rationale behind his advocacy of conservation. The best expression of this late and undeveloped addition to his thinking is in the manuscript lecture quoted from earlier, in a passage developed from journal entries of the summers of 1858 (XVII, 78 f.) and 1860 (XX, 56 f.).

The other components of Thoreau's philosophy of conservation did not exclude the possibility of a man's extracting spiritual sustenance from a nature which he neither owned nor shared in as public property but to which its holder gave him access. The new component made it difficult for Thoreau to enjoy any part of nature which had been privately acquired for the purpose of making money. It was as though the higher uses of nature could no longer be grafted on lower ones associated with acquisition and private property.

"What sort of a country," he asks, "is that where the huckleberry fields are private property?" And he answers: "When I pass such fields on the highway, my heart sinks within me, I see a blight on the land. Nature is under a veil there. I make haste away from the accursed spot. Nothing could deform her fair face more. I cannot think of it ever after but as the place where fair & palatable berries are converted into money, where the huckleberry is desecrated." In a further development of this idea, he writes: "As long as the berries are free to all comers they are beautiful, though they may be few and small, but tell me that this is a blue-berry swamp which somebody has hired, & I shall not want even to look at it."[51]

It is after this passage that Thoreau goes on to speak of the common property in nature enjoyed by the Indians and to advocate conservation in order to make up for the failure of the original settlers of New England. But he also carries the idea one step further to reach the extreme point in his critique of the industrial economy. "It is true," he writes, "we have as good a right to make berries private property, as to make wild grass & trees such—it is not worse than a thousand other practices which custom has sanctioned—but that is the worst of it, for it suggests how bad the rest are, and to what result civilisation & division of labor naturally tend, to make all things venal."[52]

The idea approached in this passage—the incompatibility between an economy of private property and aims higher than acquisition—Thoreau did not develop further. But it provides the final evidence about Thoreau's view of the coupled opposites, relation to spirit and relation to body and economy. It was the first which was absolute. In the union of principle and expediency it was the lower which was always to be accommodated to the higher.

---

[51] From "Notes on Fruits," now in the Henry W. and Albert A. Berg Collection of the New York Public Library, by whose permission it is here quoted.

[52] *Ibid.*

4

A Country to Fight For

In evaluating the economy of machines and profit which was rapidly developing in his New England, the older Thoreau continued to employ the same gauge of self-culture which he had used in his youth and by which he measured the social aspects of man's relation to nature. His goal, the simple life, still aimed at the most complete realization of the perfectibility which he believed to be innate in every person. The man who strove for it was not trying to find the way to wealth but the way "to invent and get a patent for himself" (XX, 282). At Walden, as we have seen, Thoreau sought the conditions for this simplicity in an idealized distortion of the economic order then being displaced by the industrial revolution. After his experiment failed, he moved toward a reconciliation between the simple life and the only available reality, attempting, as in his silviculture, to find a common ground for the higher and the lower. This goal he never reached. But he left behind elements of a critique of our society and intimations of an undiminishable ideal to be fought for.

I

Thoreau's resignation to the new capitalist industry cannot be as firmly documented as his acceptance of its counterpart in agriculture. Circumstance placed his home along a river with just enough current to fight off the swamp, and even after the extravagant anti-industrialism of his youth had subsided, the narrowness of his genius took him

on trips to Maine rather than to Lowell. He sought out obscure natu-
ralists, not engineers or businessmen or trade-unionists. No mention
of a strike occurs in his journal until 1858 (XVII, 238), and this first
is followed by only one other (XVIII, 82). When he saw the laboring
man it was usually as the man working for himself or as the single
hired hand, not as the labor force of a factory.

Nevertheless, we are not reduced to arguing wholly from analogy.
Directly in his comments on factories and indirectly in his reflections
on the Walden experiment, Thoreau reveals the beginnings, at least,
of an acceptance of industry as part of impersonally dictated necessity.

The first hint of this new direction is to be found early in 1851, the
day after Thoreau lectured before a Mechanics' Institute and was
taken on a tour of a gingham mill by some of his audience. His report
shows a certain breathlessness. "Saw at Clinton last night," he writes,
"a room at the gingham-mills, which covers one and seven-eighths
acres and contains 578 looms, not to speak of spindles, both throttle
and mule. The rooms all together cover three acres. They were using
between three and four hundred horse-power, and kept an engine of
two hundred horse-power, with a wheel twenty-three feet in diameter
and a band ready to supply deficiencies, which have not often occurred. Some portion of the machinery . . . revolved eighteen hundred times in a minute." He goes on to a brief description of the
manufacture, beginning with the need for long-staple cotton "clean
and free from seed" and concluding with the cloth "measured, folded,
and packed." At the end of the journal entry he writes, "I am struck
by the fact that no work has been shirked when a piece of cloth is
produced. Every thread has been counted in the finest web; it has not
been matted together. The operator has succeeded only by patience,
perseverance, and fidelity" (VIII, 134–36). About four years after this
he toured a steel mill. He noted the "vast iron rollers" between which
the heated scrap iron was reduced to long, finger-thin rods, and the
"powerful shears" which cut these rods into yard lengths. Looking
into the "cavernous furnace," he saw "the roof dripping with dark
stalactites from the mortar and bricks" (XIII, 100–102). The spirit of
these entries is certainly not the same as that which in 1839 had led
Thoreau and his brother John to row as quickly as possible past the
factories on the shores of the Merrimack, as if anxious to escape contamination.

Corresponding to this admiration of the skill and power of the productive methods of modern industry is Thoreau's recognition that there was no return to Walden. He did not fully understand why he had left the pond, and often (as he confessed in his journal) he wished himself back (IX, 214). Reporting on a walk by a favorite stream four years after the end of his experiment, he exclaimed, "To have a hut here, and a footpath to the brook!" (VIII, 455) And after another four years, in the fall of 1855, when his legs had not yet recovered from the weakness which had assailed them months earlier, he again dreamed of the old sanctuary. "I sometimes think," he wrote, "that I must go off to some wilderness where I can have a better opportunity to play life,—can find more suitable materials to build my house with, and enjoy the pleasure of collecting my fuel in the forest. I have more taste for the wild sports of hunting, fishing, wigwam-building, making garments of skin, and collecting wood wherever you find it, than for butchering, farming, carpentry, working in a factory, or going to a wood market" (XIII, 519 f.). Still later, preparing for the press the account of his second trip to Maine, he retained the statement that despite his aversion to killing he would find it a "satisfaction" to "spend a year in the woods, fishing and hunting just enough to sustain" himself, for this "would be next to living like a philosopher on the fruits of the earth you had raised"—"which also," he was still moved to admit, "attracts me" (III, 132). But despite these wishes, he stayed put in Concord.

Nor did he accept the hints and invitations of his friend Daniel Ricketson to set up a new hermitage away from Walden. When Ricketson first wrote Thoreau in 1854, he asked plainly, "Why return to 'the world' again?" He had read Thoreau's book but could not understand the cutting short of the life in the woods. It was "too true and beautiful to be abandoned for any slight reason." The Middleborough ponds near his own New Bedford, he continued, were "much more secluded than Walden, . . . really delightful places," and he offered them to Thoreau as the locale of a new experiment in simplicity.[1] Thoreau's reply ignored the question. He was interested in seeing the

---

[1] Anna and Walton Ricketson, eds., *Daniel Ricketson and His Friends* (Boston and New York, 1902), p. 28 f.

ponds, of which he had already heard, but only as certain beautiful ponds among others, not as new Waldens.[2]

In 1857 Ricketson introduced Thoreau to a young woman who planned to live alone much as he had done. Kate Brady had helped on the family farm until she was twelve, had plowed, caught fish, learned "all about farming and keeping sheep and spinning and weaving," and now she meant to return to the abandoned place and "live free." Thoreau was pleased to find that her plan was personal and not (as his had been) "professedly reformatory." But he responded neither to Kate nor to the obvious suggestion of a second retreat to a corner of a field. "All nature is my bride," he wrote in his journal (XV, 335–37).

The desire to live the life upon which Kate Brady was embarking, though apparently always present, was countered by Thoreau's acceptance of the new necessity. "I hate the present modes of living and getting a living," he exclaimed. "Farming and shopkeeping and working at a trade or profession are all odious to me. I should relish getting my living in a simple, primitive fashion" (XIV, 7). "But," he concluded, "what is the use in trying to live simply, raising what you eat, making what you wear, building what you inhabit, burning what you cut or dig, when those to whom you are allied insanely want and will have a thousand other things which neither you nor they can raise and nobody else, perchance, will pay for? The fellow-man to whom you are yoked is a steer that is ever bolting right the other way" (XIV, 8).

Side by side with the knowledge that a return to the old order was no longer possible came the realization that the preindustrial economy itself was no guarantee of a true simplicity. Thoreau illustrates this thesis in a late manuscript which appears to be part of the draft of an essay on self-culture. He has been condemning the commercial farmer, whose life, he writes, is "liable to most of the objections which have been urged against trade and commerce," for his sole aim is profit; he is a speculator, writes Thoreau, reverting to his youthful habit of punning on etymology, "and his speculum, or mirror, is a shining dollar." However, he goes on to say, "it is no better with the

---

[2] *Ibid.*, 31 f.

old fashioned farmer. I fear that his contentment is commonly stag-
nation." And he cites old Isaiah Green of Carlisle, whom we have
already met in our discussion of the surveying, a man whose surroundings had long provided all the preconditions for simplicity but
whose eighty years added up to "mere duration."[3]

In 1853, Thoreau found in a book on the Hawaiian Islands the
remark that one main obstacle to improvement there was "the ex-
tremely limited views of the natives in respect to style of living." They
were contented with so little that they had no desire for the civilization
that would bring commodities in abundance. "But this," said Thoreau, "is putting the cart before the horse, the real obstacle being their
limited views in respect to the object of living." Their simplicity of
living did not come from philosophy but from ignorance. In their
case, outward simplicity was accompanied by "idleness" and "its at-
tendant vices" and was no better than the complex life of civilized
society, and perhaps not even as good. For it is not the appearance
of simplicity which is the essential. "There are two kinds of simplicity,—one that is akin to foolishness, the other to wisdom. The
philosopher's style of living is only outwardly simple, but inwardly
complex. The savage's style of living is both outwardly and inwardly
simple. . . . It is not the tub that makes Diogenes, the Jove-born, but
Diogenes the tub" (XI, 410–12).

When Thoreau found a hut in the Acton woods, he did not, therefore, jump to the conclusion that its inhabitant was leading a truly
simple life but asked instead, "Is he insane or of sound, serene mind?
Is he weak, or is he strong?" Only if he knew "that the occupant was
a cheerful, strong, serene man" would he rejoice to see his shanty
(IX, 467).

This separation of the concept of simplicity from its original economic foundation in the preindustrial order, combined with the beginning of a new acceptance of industrial production mentioned
earlier, prepares the way for a synthesis of the aims of simplicity and
the methods of complexity, a parallel to the union of principle and

---

[3] Ms. Am. 278.5 in the Houghton Library of Harvard University, by
whose permission it is here quoted.

expediency that Thoreau attained in his silviculture. The framework for this development can be found in the dialectic of coinciding lower and higher ends illustrated in his comments on the telegraph.

Thoreau denounced the telegraph, along with the railroad and the steamboat, as an instrument by which the old subsistence farming was being debased into commercial agriculture that produced crops for the market and for profit and thus became indistinguishable from trade (XII, 108). What else, indeed, but denunciation would be consistent with his attitude toward the messages of profit and loss that the telegraph was designed to carry? At the end of August 1851 the first telegraph line through Concord was completed and Thoreau wrote characteristically in his journal that the atmosphere was full of other telegraphs and that men need not be restricted to the lines erected by people like Morse (VIII, 442). The next day he walked under the new line and "heard it vibrating like a harp high overhead. It was as the sound," he wrote, "of a far-off glorious life, a supernal life, which came down to us, and vibrated the lattice-work of this life of ours" (VIII, 450). Again and again in the years that followed he heard the divine music of the spheres through this instrument designed to serve the devil's ends. He wrote quite truly that it was not Mr. Morse who had invented *this* music (IX, 220), but he plainly recognized the possibility that given the proper ear one could detect sounds not intended by the inventor or the telegrapher. The vibrations of the telegraph wire were "like the hum of the shaft, or other machinery, of a steamboat, which at length might become music in a divine hand" (IX, 248).

In a parallel way Thoreau contradicted his attacks on the "devilish Iron Horse" of commerce with statements identifying the railroad with nature and thus with deity and self-culture. "The steam-whistle at a distance," he wrote in 1852, "sounds even like the hum of a bee in a flower. So man's works fall into nature" (X, 94). Later that year he could not "distinguish the steam of the engine toward Waltham from one of the morning fogs over hollows in the woods" (X, 299). At times the railroad became just another natural phenomenon to be included in a journal summary that might list the glumes of grass, the first lily bud, and the aroma of early white clover (XI, 235). Most significant, perhaps, is the entry of the last day of 1853: "I frequently mistake at first a very distant whistle for the higher tones of the telegraph by my side. The telegraph and railroad are closely allied, and it is fit and to be expected that at a little distance their music should be the same" (XII, 39).

But although Henry Thoreau thus began to accept the industrial mode of production, to separate his concept of simplicity from handicrafts and subsistence farming, and to sketch a framework by which simplicity might be combined with industrialism, he took no further steps than these toward the union of principle and expediency in nonagricultural production. On the contrary, side by side with these new thoughts, and continuing almost to the last page of his journals, are numerous sentences praising the arts of preindustrial life and recording Thoreau's continuing afternoon efforts to practice them.

Not long after he himself had returned to the town and abandoned all attempts at becoming an independent small producer, Thoreau began to write enthusiastic tributes to the few men of the old school still struggling for a living in out-of-the-way corners of the township. The chief subject of his praise was George Minott, an aged subsistence farmer who apparently made a personal idiosyncrasy of the localism characteristic of his group. In 1854 he told Thoreau that he had last visited Boston in 1815—and, added a Concord gossip, "had not been ten miles from home since" (XII, 175). A self-conscious opponent of commercial agriculture, Minott claimed never to have brought produce to market in his lifetime (XV, 131) and ridiculed his successful neighbor Baker who gave his own excellent corn to his stock and bought cheaper Southern corn to make bread for his family and farm hands (IX, 67). The world in which this old man had grown up was dying along with him, and the new was something he could not understand. There were still a few places in the woods that remained as they had been when he was a boy, "but for the most part," he said, "the world is turned upside down" (IX, 67). To Henry Thoreau, Minott was "perhaps the most poetical farmer," who most realized "the poetry of the farmer's life" (IX, 41).

Less frequently mentioned than Minott but at least equally praised was the old farmer and surveyor Cyrus Hubbard, the same whose compass and chain Thoreau used late in 1849 before he had acquired his own. Hubbard, writes the author of his brief memoir, "was very much attached to the way his father had done before him" and "was not very fond of new inventions, many of which did not seem to him like improvements." Like Minott, "he was attached to his home, and seldom left it for pleasure."[4] To Thoreau, as late as the end of 1856, Hubbard appeared to be the kind of independent man he had idealized in his youth, "not an office seeker" but an institution unto himself—"a system whose law is to be observed": "Moderate, natural, true, as if he were made of earth, stone, wood, snow" (XV, 144 f.).

Perhaps even more primitive than the subsistence farmers and thus more attractive to Thoreau in this mood were the men who earned their livelihood from the fish and muskrats of the Concord River or who retreated to the stream on occasion from bench and counter. There was "always to be seen either some unshaven wading man, an old mower of the river meadows, familiar with water, vibrating his long pole over the lagoons of the off-shore pads, or else some solitary fisher, in a boat behind the willows, like a mote in the sunbeams reflecting the light" (VIII, 321). And along the shore were the musquash-hunters, those "aboriginal men," "keeping the same rank and savage hold" on life that their predecessors had for endless generations. A few of them, like one-eyed John Goodwin, and Sudbury Haynes of the old coat that was "much patched, with many colors," and "the dark-faced trapper" George Melvin, followed by his "lank, bluish-white, black-spotted hound," emerge from the anonymity Thoreau usually reserved for his townsmen.[5] But significantly it is only their hunter or fisherman that emerges, not their whole selves. Like Minott and Hubbard they are less men than symbols.

Consistent with this approval of subsistence agriculture and its adjunct hunting and fishing are the journal passages in praise of the handicraft manufacture which was their historical counterpart. One

---

[4] Rebecca Wetherbee, "Memoir of Cyrus Hubbard," in *Memoirs of Members of the Social Circle in Concord, 2d Series, from 1795 to 1840* (Cambridge, Massachusetts, 1888), p. 192 f.

[5] IX, 290; XV, 148; XVII, 422 f., 425.

winter on his way to a lecture engagement in New Hampshire Thoreau had to go into a shop to warm himself, and he thought the incident worth recording, for there was a tub and pail maker who did his work "by hand, splitting out the staves with a curved knife and smoothing them with curved shaves" (XV, 187). Later, in Concord, where he was an occasional visitor at Barrett's sawmill, he noticed the miller's apprentice making birch and maple trays and was "pleased with the sight of the trays because the tools used were so simple" and because they were "made by hand, not by machinery." The relation between the apprentice and his work he called "poetic" (XVII, 227). As late as 1860 he remarked on a little boy "who had on a home-made cap of a woodchuck-skin, which his father or elder brother had killed and cured, and his mother or elder sister had fashioned into a nice warm cap." "Such," he declared, "should be the history of every piece of clothing we wear" (XIX, 166).

As if to complete the picture, Thoreau exhibited in the fifties a distinct interest in the economic activities of preindustrial New England. In 1854, for example, he got hold of an old account book found in some deacon's attic. On the cover, "amid many marks and scribblings," was the inscription, "Mr. Ephraim Jones His Wast Book, Anno Domini 1742." The old ledger occupied him about a week. He went through it entry by entry, astonished by the changes which had overtaken Concord since they were written. "Methinks," he wrote, "my genius is coeval with that time."[6] And even as late as the fall of 1860 he was much impressed by a few old stone weights seen in a museum, for he loved "to see anything that implies a simpler mode of life and greater nearness to the earth" (XX, 88).

Thoreau not only praised the primitive arts of life but practiced them as well. He spoke with particular approval of the fact that Minott had a wood lot in which he felled his own trees and thus provided his own fuel. It seemed to him to be "more economical, as well as more poetical, to have a woodlot and cut and get out your own wood from year to year than to buy it at your door" (XV, 178). Thoreau never owned a wood lot, but when he wrote this sentence at the end of 1856 he had for several years been collecting much of his own fire-

---

[6] XII, 77 ff., 94 ff.

wood from forest and river and had made the gathering of fuel a regular activity of his autumn.

Together with collecting fuel belong other experiments of the post-Walden years in which for a given moment and over a small area of his life he once again followed the pattern of George Minott. He made his own maple sugar (XIV, 207 ff.). He tried to eat acorns, both raw and cooked (IX, 56–59). In *Walden* he tells of the ground nut which he had discovered in the fall of 1852 and whose tubers he had eaten "roasted and boiled at supper time" (X, 384). In the day of market agriculture, "of fatted cattle and waving grain-fields," this "humble root" had been forgotten, but to Thoreau it seemed like "a faint promise of Nature to rear her own children and feed them simply here at some future period" (II, 264).

The paradox that Thoreau thus presents, of a movement toward the acceptance of the industrial mode of production contradicted by praise and practice of economic activities that antedate it, can be explained by two facts. The first is that the social philosophy which had equipped him to build his hut and plant his beans by the shore of Walden was not immediately eliminated by the failure of its practice but lingered past its day to engage in rear-guard skirmish with its successor. In an earlier chapter we have seen it still operating in Thoreau's moonlight communications with nature, the antithesis of his daytime research in the silvical foundation for a union of principle and expediency. In his relation to industry as well, the old view persisted, a reverberating echo of the Walden experiment.

But the tenacity of this persistence can be explained only by the second fact: that the reconciliation between the simple life and the industrial mode of production which Thoreau groped for was a goal beyond his reaching. The essential reason for this was that Thoreau was unable to discover any germs in the industrialism he knew that would in maturity carry it beyond the division of labor classically described by Adam Smith and beyond the motive of acquisition. So long as industry could not transcend the division of labor which resulted in the division of men and so long as it was aimed at ends which were external, Thoreau would never be able to reconcile it with the integral development of the whole person which was essential to his doctrine of self-culture.

II

Thoreau's inability to rid himself of this paradox resulted in the concurrent existence of two concepts of simplicity. The first, which he described explicitly, accepted the incompatibility between the actual economic life of his time and the higher goal of self-culture and preached a divided life. Thoreau himself, if we neglect the other face of his paradox, provides an excellent example of this sort of simplicity. He made his living as a surveyor, part of the machinery, that is, for the definition and exchange of property rights and an essential member of a community devoted to acquisition. But denying this aim and practicing voluntary poverty, he strove (with unequal success) to limit his surveying to the mornings and to devote the greater part of his time to the activities whose end product was his essays.

In a journal entry of the fall of 1857, he generalizes from his own experience to provide this concept with a theory. "Every one who deserves to be regarded as higher than the brute," he writes, "may be supposed to have an earnest purpose, to accomplish which is the object of his existence, and this is at once his work and his supremest pleasure." But the economy does not, for the most part, allow a man to earn his living by an activity that will further this object; hence he must divide his life between his true work and making a living. And since it is the former which demands the greatest energies, Thoreau called the latter an amusement: "for diversion and relaxation, for suggestion and education and strength, there is offered the never-failing amusement of getting a living." But it is never-failing only when "temperately indulged in." "Farming and building and manufacturing and sailing," he declares, "are the greatest and wholesomest amusements that were ever invented (for God invented them), and I suppose that the farmers and mechanics know it, only I think they indulge to excess generally, and so what was meant for joy becomes the sweat of the brow." And later: "I have aspired to practice in succession all the honest arts of life, that I may gather all their fruits. But then, if you are intemperate, if you toil to raise an unnecessary amount of corn, even the large crop of wheat becomes as a small crop of chaff" (XVI, 145–47).

What we have here is the combination of voluntary poverty with the practice, as often as possible, of the primitive economic arts. The poverty, as at Walden, was a necessary consequence once acquisition was rejected and a maximum amount of energy devoted to the higher goal of self-culture. Thoreau practiced it with moderation and wrote of it in his journal with polemic excess, reaching at times the questionable principle that "just in proportion to the outward poverty is the inward wealth" (IX, 114 f.).

It is statements such as this that reveal the concept's chief weakness. There was of course, to begin with, the fact that the majority had no real choice about the number of hours that they spent in the shop or store or factory and the number they might devote to self-culture. But there was the additional danger that the outward appearance of simplicity would become an end in itself, a symbol of an inward richness whose presence would simply be assumed. A suggestion of this, as has been mentioned, is to be found in Thoreau's accounts of the old farmers and of Concord's vagrant hunters and fishermen. A more complete illustration is in his praise of the farmer Reuben Rice.

Rice's life, declares Thoreau, is "poetic." The man "has learned that rare art of living, the very elements of which most professors do not know." He has tools of all kinds which he has made himself, and whenever possible he does his own work rather than hire it out. He works slowly, taking pleasure in his craftsmanship, "enjoying the sweet of it." But he does not labor to excess, and in good weather goes out with his sons to hunt or fish or to follow bees to their hive for the honey. His sons gather stumps for firewood and skin the woodchucks shot or trapped on their farm to make mittens.

But this same Rice, it turns out, is a man who "by good sense and calculation . . . has become rich" and has "invested his property well." He owns not only a home in Concord Center and a farm and bean fields in Sudbury but houses in Boston, "whose repair he attends to, finds tenants for them, and collects the rent." He "dwells not in untidy luxury," but he obviously need not worry that his fishing or bee hunting will seriously affect his prosperity. To praise Rice, Thoreau has to strike an unusual balance between the lower law and the higher: "Though he owned all Beacon Street, you might find that his mittens were made of the skin of a woodchuck that had ravaged his bean-field, which he had cured."[7] Here the first concept of simplicity approaches its limit: a fetishism in which occasional practice of the arts of primitive life becomes a religious ritual granting absolution for days devoted to low ends.

That the echo of the Walden experiment persisted long enough to reach this self-defeating excess is to be explained, as has been said, by Thoreau's inability to effect a reconciliation between the simple life and the industrial mode of production. Also contributing to this result was the fact that Thoreau wrote about the economy as an artist and not as a social scientist. His need was for the concrete, and the only concrete approximations of simplicity available were in handicrafts and subsistence agriculture. To understand the second concept of simplicity, we must abstract its categories from the forms in which the artist Thoreau illustrated them.

The keystone of the doctrine of simplicity is the principle of self-culture. At the end of his career as at the beginning, Thoreau believed that "the object of life is something else than acquiring property" (XVII, 196), that the man approaching success is not he who has got "much money, many houses and barns and woodlots," but he who has been "trying to better his condition in a higher sense than this, has been trying to invent something, to be somebody,—*i.e.*, to invent and get a patent for himself" (XX, 281 f.). This insistence on the primacy of mind and soul, with its complemental rejection of acquisition, was expressed by Thoreau most completely in relation to nature and to agriculture and has already been described on earlier pages. But there can be no doubt that he intended self-culture to be a measure of other economic activities as well. "The value of any experience," he declared in a late manuscript, "is measured, of course, not by the amount of money, but the amount of development we get out of it."[8]

Inseparable from self-culture in its later stage as in the earlier was the ideal of an integral existence, in which there would be no division

---

[7] XIV, 26 f.; XV, 289.

[8] "Notes on Fruits: Four Pages Holograph," in the Henry W. and Albert A. Berg Collection of the New York Public Library, by whose permission it is here quoted.

between labor for the body and labor for the spirit. The economic
activities which assist in perfecting the unique contribution of a man's
character Thoreau termed life in the present, distinguishing them
from all those others which merely sustain the body and are postpone-
ments of life's proper business. The distinction between them he illustrated by the analogy of the artist and the artisan. He noticed one
evening a horse which during the day powered a sawing machine
through a treadmill and was let out at night to graze: at each step
the animal lifted his hind legs "convulsively high from the ground,
as if the whole earth were a treadmill continually slipping away from
under him while he climbed its convex surface." To Thoreau the
horse was "symbolical of the moral condition . . . of all artisans in
contradistinction from artists, all who are engaged in any routine; for
to them also the whole earth is a treadmill, and the routine instantly
results in a similar painful deformity. The horse may bear the mark
of his servitude on the muscles of his legs, the man on his brow" (XI,
276 f.). The ideal which he had in mind, and which he could not
find in production based on division of labor, was an economy whose
workers would no longer be mere artisans.

Thoreau kept returning to the activities of a more primitive economy because only there could he find that wholeness of relationship
betwen a man and his work whose highest realization is in the life of
the artist. One March day he found an Indian basket woven of osiers.
The man who was "weaving that creel," he wrote, "was meditating
a small poem in his way. It was equal to a successful stanza whose
subject was spring" (XVI, 313 f.). Considered abstractly, a subsistence economy in which the individual does not produce commodities
for exchange but only articles for his own consumption provides the
condition under which a man may always be an artist. For the true
craftsman, like the artist, conceives his task in its entirety, selects the
raw materials, and transforms them into the article which had been
foreseen from the beginning. Artistic activity of this kind, not aimed
at the market, becomes an end in itself, and through it the man disci-
plines and develops his own mind at the same time that he is matur-
ing its product. With the division of labor, the productive process is
separated into stages and each man acts upon the raw materials in only
one stage or in several at most, and the task of conceiving the cycle of

production and viewing it in its totality becomes itself a stage and the province of a specialist. The individual producer cannot maintain his relation to the productive process as a whole or make his labor an end in itself. He does not produce articles for consumption but commodities for sale and must exchange the products of his specialized labor in order to obtain the necessities of life. His daily work is thus no longer life in the present, but postponed life, and if he wishes to develop the potentialities of his soul he must do so after hours. Moreover, felt Thoreau, it was the division of labor that was the cause, in his time, of the devotion to profit which closed men's eyes to self-culture; it tended, as he said in a passage already quoted, "to make all things venal."

In addition to making possible self-culture through the restoration of a creative relationship between man and labor, Thoreau sought the elimination of a certain depersonalizing of economic relations which he associated with the replacement of barter by business transactions and of the relation between man and man by that between man and market. "How rarely," he exclaimed in his journal, are we "encouraged by the sight of simple actions in the street! We deal with banks and other institutions, where the life and humanity are concealed,—what there is. I like at least to see the great beams half exposed in the ceiling or the corner" (XIX, 169).

These ideals Thoreau was never able to combine with the methods of production insisted on by his contemporaries. The failure of the Walden experiment had cut the doctrine of simplicity off from any economic foundation. Thoreau could no longer advise mankind to resign from the industrial and agricultural revolutions and head for the woods. Neither, however, could he reconcile his individualism with any form of socialism. He was left with a critique of industrial and commercial civilization but with no associated program of action. His concept of simplicity became, like the Old Marlborough Road, "a direction out there" (V, 215), away from the definable evils of the social order but with no clear goal in sight.

The audiences at his lectures, their practical American minds looking for a program, complained that they could not understand him. All they could find was the obviously unbelievable implication that mankind should return to the life of the savage. Thoreau's friend

Ricketson, constituting himself their spokesman, asked the lecturer why, "having common sense," he did not "write in plain English always" and "*teach* men in detail how to live a simpler life." Thoreau replied that he was not interested in giving men instructions but in inspiring them with ideals. "As a preacher," he wrote, "I should be prompted to tell men, not so much how to get their wheat bread cheaper, as of the bread of life compared with which *that* is bran. . . . Don't spend your time in drilling soldiers, who may turn out hirelings after all, but give to undrilled peasantry a *country* to fight for" (VI, 259 f.).

III

The realization that there was no ideal society waiting just around the corner required of Thoreau a new approach to the economic evils of his time. In the Walden period and in the aspect of his later years represented by "Life Without Principle," he assumed that people lived a life they had chosen and that a new one was to be had for the trying. If men did not take advantage of their freedom to clothe themselves in a new society it was the consequence of their own baseness. Now, as part of him began to accept America as it was, he thought less of ideal social orders and more of specific improvements within the society that had been given him.

The change is perhaps most easily illustrated in Thoreau's attitude to the Irish. In his youth, advocacy of self-reliance and a willingness to see more freedom in Concord than really existed led Thoreau to disapprove of charity to these exploited immigrants. The function of the reformer was not to find a helping dollar but to make his own life an example by which the impoverished might be inspired to transform themselves. For if the internal moral revolution was actually within reach, why waste energy modifying what was only on the outside? "There are a thousand hacking at the branches of evil to one who is striking at the root," he declared in the chronologically earliest chapter of *Walden*, "and it may be that he who bestows the largest amount of time and money on the needy is doing the most by his mode of life to produce that misery which he strives in vain to relieve" (II, 84).

It was in this spirit that Thoreau lectured John Field during his second month at Walden, when a sudden rain led him to take shelter under that poor man's leaking roof. Hard-working Field was redeeming a wet meadow for a Concord farmer in exchange for a little money and the right to grow a single crop, and in his ignorance he did not know how poor a bargain he had struck. But instead of making suggestions that might improve Field's mean reality, Thoreau told him all about the Walden experiment (VII, 383 f.). Even as late as 1850, pained at seeing little Johnny Riordan growing up in a shack, he tried to ease himself with the belief that this "more interesting child than usual" had the internal resources to overcome environment and to extract from shanty poverty a "greater independence" and "closeness to nature" than he might have drawn from other surroundings (VIII, 116 f.).

How different is his exclamation two years later, when in the middle of the coldest winter in two decades he sees Johnny with "one thickness only of ragged cloth sewed on to his pantaloons over his little shirt, and shoes with large holes in the toes, into which the snow got." "Is man so cheap," demands Thoreau, that this boy "cannot be clothed but with a mat or a rag? that we should abandon to him our *worn-out* clothes or our *cold* victuals? Infancy pleads with equal eloquence from all platforms. Rather let the mature rich wear the rags and insufficient clothing, the infant poor and rich, if any, wear the costly furs, the purple and fine linen. Our charitable institutions are an insult to humanity,—a charity which dispenses the crumbs that fall from its overloaded tables! whose waste and whose example helped to produce that poverty!" (IX, 242 n.–244 n.)

Thoreau helped Johnny Riordan in the ways that were open to him. He had earlier given a pair of pants to be cut down for the boy (IX, 241), and in this bitter winter of 1852 brought him a new coat (IX, 289). More important, he gathered his journal comments on Johnny and combined them into what appears to have been part of an intended lecture. It is from this composition, whose date is unestablished, that we have quoted Thoreau's denunciation of the mistreatment of the poor.

In an essentially similar way Thoreau reacted to two accidents that took place near Concord in the fifties, one in a gunpowder plant, the other on the railroad, not waiting for new men or a new society but painfully sharing the sufferings of the men that were and striving to ameliorate their lot within the society that existed.

The explosion at the American Company's powder mill in Acton occurred early in January 1853, on a morning when Thoreau happened to be in the house, and he was at the scene in about forty minutes, gathering details from earlier arrivals and looking about for himself. His initial account (of which more later) is terse. "Some of the clothes of the men were in the tops of the trees, where undoubtedly their bodies had been and left them. The bodies were naked and black, some limbs and bowels here and there, and a head at a distance from its trunk. The feet were bare; the hair singed to a crisp" (X, 455). His intense emotion lies behind the observing eye and takes the reader unawares.

Two days later Thoreau sought to exorcise the evil by concentrating on the vibration of the telegraph wire. "This wire is my redeemer," he wrote hopefully. "Day before yesterday I looked at the mangled and blackened bodies of men which had been blown up by powder, and felt that the lives of men were not innocent, and that there was an avenging power in nature. Today I hear this immortal melody, while the west wind is blowing balmily on my cheek, and methinks a roseate sunset is preparing. Are there not two powers?" (X, 459.) But these wish-fulfilling truths did not prove satisfactory. Some two weeks later he dreamed of "delving amid the graves of the dead" and soiling his fingers with their "rank mould." He explained the dream by the influence of "the rottenness of human relations," which had so recently appeared to him "full of death and decay, and offended the nostrils" (X, 472).

Several months later the slow-moving Assabet River had begun carrying burned timbers into the Concord. "And some, no doubt," wrote Thoreau, "were carried down to the Merrimack, and by the Merrimack to the ocean, till perchance they got into the Gulf Stream and were cast up the coast of Norway, covered with barnacles, or who can tell what more distant strand?—still bearing some traces of burnt powder, still capable of telling how and where they were launched, to those who can read their signs. To see a man lying all bare, lank, and tender on the rocks, like a skinned frog or lizard! We did not suspect that he was made of such cold, tender, clammy substance before" (XI, 211 f.). Echoes of this trauma appear in the journal as late as 1859 (XVII, 396).

If we return now to the initial account, we will witness Thoreau surveying the scene as a man interested in reducing the extent of future explosions. He first identifies the kernel mill in which the original explosion had taken place and then surveys the other buildings to determine the extent of their damage and the distance of each from the kernel mill. Following this, he ascertains as well the limit to which the burning timbers had been thrown. "Put the different buildings thirty rods apart," he concludes, "and then but one will blow up at a time" (X, 455). The lives of the powder workers cannot wait for the rearrangement of rotten human relations.

Of parallel significance in the development of Thoreau's relation to the economy was the accidental killing of a man at a railroad bridge, "the fatal Lincoln Bridge," early in December of 1856 (XV, 151). The crossing had been up some ten years and had already taken at least ten lives, but nothing had been done about it, and for Thoreau it therefore became a symbol of the inhumanity of the entire profit-centered economy. In a passage that deserves to be anthologized along with the many other small masterpieces lying neglected in the journals, he celebrates the American efficiency and neatness with which this executioner has performed its job.

"Yesterday," he writes a week after the accident, "I walked under the murderous Lincoln Bridge, where at least ten men have been swept dead from the cars within as many years. I looked to see if their heads had indented the bridge, if there were sturdy blows given as well as received, and if their brains lay about. But I could see neither the one nor the other. The bridge is quite uninjured, even, and straight, not even the paint worn off or discolored. The ground is clean, the snow spotless, and the place looks as innocent as a bank whereon the wild thyme grows. It does its work in an artistic manner" (XV, 175).

From the heartlessness of the economy he turns then to attack its hypocritical morality. "The days of the gallows," he announces, "are numbered." The next time the county has to execute a criminal they have only to hire him out to the railroad. "Let the priest accompany him to the freight-train, pray with him, and take leave of him there." The gallows, after all, "bears an ill name, and I think deservedly. No doubt it has hung many an innocent man, but this Lincoln Bridge, long as it has been in our midst and busy as it has been, no legislature, nobody, indeed, has ever seriously complained of, unless it was some bereaved mother, who was naturally prejudiced against it." It has, moreover, another advantage, "an advantage to the morals of the community, that, strange as it may seem, no crowd ever assembles at this spot; there are no morbidly curious persons, no hardened reprobates, no masculine women, no anatomists there" (XV, 176).

As with the explosion at the powder plant, Thoreau has a life-saving practical suggestion. If this "monster . . . could be held back only four feet from where he now crouches, all travellers might pass in safety and laugh him to scorn." And this, he goes on to say, "would require but a little resolution in our legislature" (XV, 175 f.). Instead of projecting ideal people whose rounded lives correspond with the orb of the oversoul, Thoreau is here trying to cut down actual human suffering. Not man as he should be, but man as he can be.

5

Action and Inaction

The evolution of Thoreau's mature approach to American society proceeded unevenly, as was said earlier, along three lines. Two of these we have already examined. In his research on forests, and to a lesser extent in his comments on industry and on the simple life, Thoreau succeeded in glimpsing a path toward the ideal that led through the real. He showed New Englanders that the way to wealth in managing wood lots could also be the way to preserve the forest for spiritual uses. And he took a long step toward the view that the implements associated with economic complexity might in time be made to serve the ideals of simplicity.

In both of these areas he discovered as well that the protection of the spiritual interest of the many might require curtailment of the material interest of the few. The farmer who could not see beyond the sale of his next harvest must be taught by a forest warden to accept a perennial crop that would keep putting money in his pocket and would also preserve the woodland for those who made a higher use of it than he did. The man who wished to monopolize a river bank or a hilltop or a roadside must be prevented from doing so by the action of local and federal government, whose responsibility it is to give mankind access to nature. The industrialist or railroad owner who rushed toward his profit heedless of the lives of others must be told where to place his shops and his trestles. In his approach to both industry and agriculture, Thoreau was being compelled, that is, not only to accept a union between principle and expediency but to recognize that the success of the single man in his private life was dependent on the success of the community of men in their social life. He was moving toward the point at which he could no longer argue as in "Civil Disobedience" that government "can have no pure right over my person and property but what I concede to it" (IV, 387).

There seems always to have been a corner of his mind that granted the necessity of government. When he refused to pay the tax symbolizing allegiance to a state that sanctioned slavery, he could add, "I have never declined paying the highway tax, because I am as desirous of being a good neighbor as I am of being a bad subject" (IV, 380). It was government of man's periphery rather than his center, of areas ruled only by expediency. Economy itself had always been central, associated with the ideal of the integral life all of whose elements contribute to self-culture. But so long as Thoreau thought it necessary to erect an atomistic community outside the established economic order, he could avoid association with the legislatures that helped govern it. Now that he was beginning to accept the principle that the ideal of self-culture had to be attained not outside industrial society but within it and by means of it, matters that had earlier been peripheral were being forced into the center. The new view of industry and of agriculture demanded a new view of government and of political action. First, it required a solution of the problem which Thoreau had avoided when he washed his hands of slavery: how to achieve that union with political expediency which will gain popular support for political principle. Second, it demanded that he give up the no-organizationist's reliance on spontaneous parallel individual actions and learn to participate in reform and political organization.

At this point in Thoreau's intellectual growth his relation to the antislavery movement became critical. His starting point in political theory, as we have seen, was the peculiar anarchism of the no-organization abolitionists, and to overcome the persistence of this ingrained ideology required massive pressure from outside the man to reinforce the spontaneous growth within him. But the great reform movements which sought to control the excesses of our economy did not arise until after the Civil War. In only one aspect of Thoreau's America was this external reinforcement available: in the struggle to abolish slavery.

It seems clear in retrospect that the movement which brought about the abolition of slavery matured only in proportion as it was able to combine the high ideal of freedom with the low ideal of self-interest, whether the latter involved land or markets or control of the federal government. It seems equally clear that this developing union of principle and expediency found its characteristic expression in political action and political parties, in the line that led from the Liberty Party through the Free Soil Party to the Republican Party. If Thoreau, before the end of the Civil War, was to discover a politics complementary to his economics, it would be through involvement with this movement. Such an involvement he did not wholly achieve.

The pattern of Thoreau's relation to antislavery after his return from the pond can be epitomized in the contrast between the young man arrested alone of a midsummer for nonpayment of taxes, his own hero, and Captain John Brown, in whom Thoreau revered at last the militant he could not be. In 1846 he had been put into jail as he was going to get a shoe repaired, and when released the next morning he returned to the shoemaker and then walked away from town and government to the berry fields, smugly mended in soul and gear. Thirteen years later he wrote of those who could not understand John Brown that "they must enlarge themselves to conceive of him. . . . a man who did not wait till he was personally interfered with or thwarted in some harmless business before he gave his life to the cause of the oppressed" (IV, 424). It was this enlargement that he had himself experienced.

John Brown had been incipient in Thoreau's thinking almost from the beginning. He was the opposite of that Brahman of *A Week* who "never proposes courageously to assault evil, but patiently to starve it out" (I, 146). When Thoreau called him Christ he was thus not falling back on the handiest symbol but using one that had long been awaiting its embodiment, for it was Christ who faced the Brahman in the original antithesis.

But here we have less development than a leap from one pole to its already existing opposite—or, to be more accurate, the adoption of one extreme after Thoreau's failure to compromise the conflict between quietist and militant in his personality. Whoever studies the journals and letters and essays that separate the printing of "Civil

Disobedience" from the arrest of John Brown will therefore find very little on slavery and politics. The record of those ten years, so voluminous and informative, as we have seen, on the evolution of Thoreau's attitude to the forest, can tell us very little of this other process, which was not correspondingly accretional. Only on two occasions did Thoreau feel so closely touched by events as to seek an audience for his thoughts.

I

The first of these was the enforced return of the fugitive Thomas Sims to Georgia and slavery. Sims had fled bondage one winter night by stowing away on a brig at dock in Savannah. Two weeks later, just outside the sanctuary of Boston, he was discovered and locked in a cabin but broke out, stole the ship's small boat, and rowed himself to freedom. Or so he thought. Foolishly telegraphing home, he betrayed his address, and within a very few days the rice planter who claimed his person had dispatched an agent northward. On April 3, 1851, Sims was arrested as a runaway and brought before the commissioner locally authorized to enforce the Fugitive Slave Law.[1]

Not two months earlier, another handcuffed fugitive had been brought into the Federal Court House in Boston only to be taken out almost immediately by a crowd of free Negroes and hidden away in West Cambridge. A few weeks later he was brought to Concord in the middle of the night and from there taken one step closer to Canada and freedom by one of Thoreau's neighbors.[2]

Thomas Sims, however, was not as fortunate as Shadrach. The night of his arrest he was clapped into the Court House and the building surrounded with chains and soldiers. Forced thus to fall back on lawyers, the abolitionists argued the unconstitutionality of the Fugitive Slave Law and took advantage of every legal opening in their

---

[1] A detailed account is Leonard W. Levy, "Sims' Case: the Fugitive Slave Law in Boston in 1851," *Journal of Negro History,* XXXV (January 1950), 39–74.

[2] Edward Channing, *A History of the United States* (6 vols.; New York, 1926), VI, 106; Ralph Korngold, *Two Friends of Man* (Boston, 1950), p. 218.

effort to free Sims and preserve Boston from the stigma of slave-catching. In retrospect we can see that it was probably too soon to expect anything but what happened. There was no aroused public of free men to lift the judges' eyes from the letter of the law, and on April 12, 1851, Thomas Sims was returned to slavery.

Henry Thoreau was not in the small group whose vigilance brought it to the dock at four that morning to witness the rendition. The representative of Concord there whom he later singled out for praise was the minister Daniel Foster, and Thoreau learned of Foster's dockside prayer by reading of it (VIII, 176). Later that day he went about his surveying. His "Field Notes" also show him to have worked at his trade at the onset of the crisis, on the fourth and fifth days of April, when he was plotting land for one James McCafferty.[3] For the rest, the record is bare.

He neither wrote nor received any letter we know of.[4] A floral calendar that includes this season has no entries between March 30 and April 22.[5] The journal, in which he was then writing only on occasion and often without dates, includes only two brief sentences and a single irrelevant quotation that might possibly belong to this period (VIII, 172 f.). Nor does his name appear in the diary of Bronson Alcott, who was in Boston all through the affair, a member of the Vigilance Committee, and who recorded conversations with people who meant less to him personally than did Thoreau.[6]

But though he most likely did not journey to Boston for the meetings and milling about of that trying week, Thoreau derived from it at least one lesson that the experience itself could have given: the knowledge that large numbers of men and women were ready to defy the government on an issue of conscience. No longer did he find it necessary, as in "Civil Disobedience," to look only to the rare single

---

[3] "Field Notes of Surveys," pp. 45, 50.

[4] Walter Harding and Carl Bode, "Henry David Thoreau: A Check List of His Correspondence," *Bulletin of the New York Public Library,* LIX (May 1955), 238.

[5] "Order of Flowers Accidentally Observed in '51," in the Huntington Libr: ry, by whose permission it is here used.

[6] Odell Shepard, ed., *The Journals of Bronson Alcott* (Boston, 1938), pp. 2 |3–46.

man who had hired or squatted somewhere on a small plot and whom lack of self-interest thus made free to follow higher law (IV, 373). Nor did he feel, as before, the need to declare that "there is but little virtue in the action of masses of men" (IV, 363).

On the contrary. Forced to choose between the verdict of jurists and the spontaneous aggressiveness of antislavery New Englanders, he threw in his lot with the latter. He would not trust the life of the fugitive "to the judges of all the Supreme Courts in the world put together, to be sacrificed or saved by precedent." He "would much rather trust to the sentiment of the people, which would itself be a precedent to posterity." The judges could not be relied on to glimpse absolute truth because their legality was premised on outdated institutions. It was necessary for the people, who spoke from the heart and not from anachronisms, to "go behind the courts" (VIII, 177 f.).

The effect of such action, however, must be "to some extent fatal to the courts" (VIII, 178)—and for this Henry Thoreau was quite ready. Behind the infusion of populism into his concept of the operation of higher law was the long-standing conviction that his was a moment fit only for revolution. In "Civil Disobedience," when he was thinking chiefly of "a peaceable revolution" effected by the passive resistance of all just men, he had left place for a further step if this should fail. "When the subject has refused allegiance, and the officer has resigned his office, then the revolution is accomplished," he had written. "But even suppose blood should flow," he immediately added. "Is there not a sort of blood shed when the conscience is wounded?" (IV, 371) By 1851, he had already begun to think of blood and the further step.

In looking to war, however, as in refusing to pay the tax, he was almost completely isolated. "I do not believe," he wrote, "that the North will soon come to blows with the South on this question. It would be too bright a page to be written in the history of the race at present" (VIII, 174). He retreated, therefore, to his earlier tactics. Just as in his concept of simplicity he clung to a condemnation of the "complex" life which strings middlemen between an individual and his economic necessities, so in politics he persisted in searching for a strategy that would enable a singly-acting person to bring his enmity to bear directly on the slave power and on its Northern supporters.

Leaving no room, then, for the attempt to reach at evil indirectly through ballots and legislatures, Thoreau suggests—among other tactics that he refers to but does not identify—violation of the Fugitive Slave Law and a boycott of all newspapers that fail to oppose the enforcement of that law.

It is perhaps an accident of imagery that he refers to the price of a paper as a "tax" and writes that to kill these papers off, the antislavery men of New England have only to "withhold their cents" (VIII, 179 f.). But more likely it is evidence of the substitution of a new symbolic act for the withholding of taxes which he had advocated in vain several years earlier. One element in Thoreau is still washing its hands of slavery. The other is looking about for individual actions that will anticipate the direct assault. Shortly after the Sims affair there was an election in Massachusetts, and Emerson spoke to Thoreau's ideal subsistence farmer about casting a vote. George Minott, he recorded in his journal, "thinks that it is of no use balloting, for it will not stay, but what you do with the gun will stay so."[7] It does not seem unlikely that Minott and Thoreau were of one mind.

Of the two specific tactics recommended by Thoreau—violation of the Fugitive Slave Law and refusal to buy compromising newspapers—it is probably safe to assume that he rather consistently practiced the second, for there is no evidence that he had as yet begun to subscribe even to the *Weekly Tribune*, which shortly afterward became his staple. But for a man who had indeed never been much of a newspaper reader, this was hardly even a Lenten sacrifice.

Of the Fugitive Slave Law, Thoreau wrote at this time that a person "need not go out of his way" to trample it "under foot" (VIII, 177). Partly, he was jibing at the Garrisonians, who at a meeting in Concord on April 3 had declared that they would "trample" that law, "now and for ever, utterly under our feet,"[8] and who were using similar phrases in resolutions adopted elsewhere.[9] What he meant—disregarding, as was his custom, the rituals essential to a mass move-

---

[7] Edward W. Emerson and Waldo E. Forbes, eds., *Journals of Ralph Waldo Emerson* (10 vols.; Boston and New York, 1912), VIII, 206.

[8] *Liberator,* XXI (April 18, 1851), 58.

[9] At Weymouth, for example, on March 30, for which see *Liberator,* XXI (April 4, 1851), 55.

ment—was that a man who strove to live by principle did not have to pass a resolution to do so but would in the normal course of his life violate a law whose "natural habitat is in the dirt" (VIII, 177). And there can be no doubt that whenever Thoreau chanced to be in a position to aid a fugitive he did so.

But it was apparently his family and not Thoreau himself that formed a recognized part of the Concord station of the Underground Railroad. Mrs. Edwin Bigelow, one of the participants, told Edward Waldo Emerson in 1892 that while Thoreau lived in the woods, fugitives—Thoreau in *Walden* credits himself with but one (II, 169)— were sometimes brought to him for safekeeping. However, she added, the cabin was not designed for concealment, and Thoreau more commonly guided the slave to his father's house or to some other safe place in town. Once in the Thoreau house, it was Mrs. Thoreau who determined what was to be done, and her son became only a helper. In this capacity, however, he contributed much by buying tickets at the railway station, accompanying fugitives to the train, and sitting in the same car with them as guard, though not so close as to attract eyes to their association.[10]

The little evidence now available tends to support Mrs. Bigelow's assertions. Thoreau's journal for October 1, 1851, gives a brief account of a runaway slave named Henry Williams whom Thoreau had late that afternoon put on the train for Canada. Williams had been living in Boston for about a year when he heard that agents of his former master were after him, and he walked the score of miles to Concord in the night, bringing letters to the Thoreau family from Garrison and from the abolitionist pastor Joseph C. Lovejoy. Money was immediately collected to send him on his way, and Thoreau went off at noon to buy his ticket. But at the depot he saw a man "who looked and behaved so much like a Boston policeman" that he returned home and waited for a later train (IX, 37 f.).

Similarly, Moncure D. Conway reports that the day after he was first introduced to Thoreau, in the summer of 1853, he came to the Thoreaus' house to find a fugitive "who had come fainting to their

---

[10] Edward Waldo Emerson's manuscript account of his interview with Mrs. Edwin Bigelow, December 13, 1892, now in the possession of Mr. Raymond Emerson, with whose kind permission it is here used.

door about daybreak and thrown himself on their mercy." Thoreau could not take his customary walk that day, but had to stand guard and care for his charge. The man "must be fed, his swollen feet bathed, and he must think of nothing but rest. Again and again," writes Conway, "this coolest and calmest of men drew nearer to the trembling negro, and bade him feel at home, and have no fear that any power should again wrong him."[11]

It is in the nature of such an activity as aiding fugitives that details and quantities should be always difficult and often impossible to establish. Mrs. Bigelow reported that Thoreau went as escort probably more often than any other man in Concord, but just what this would mean in a town noted for the fact that most of its few abolitionists were women it is now impossible to tell. Channing was undoubtedly right when he said that "not one slave alone was expedited to Canada by Thoreau's personal assistance."[12] The historian of the Underground Railroad in Massachusetts, however, does not seem to have found any more evidence than that already cited, and there is no reason to challenge his conclusion that Thoreau was only an "occasional" participant.[13]

---

[11] "Thoreau," *Fraser's Magazine,* LXXIII (April 1866), 460 f. A similar account is in Conway's *Autobiography: Memoirs and Experiences* (2 vols.; Boston and New York, 1904), I, 141. If it were not that Conway met Thoreau for the first time in 1853, the slave described here might well be Henry Williams. Conway writes that he and the fugitive recognized each other, having met before in the South, and Thoreau reports that Williams had fled from Stafford County, Virginia, which was Conway's home county (Mary E. Burtis, *Moncure Conway, 1832–1907* [New Brunswick, New Jersey, 1952], p. 3). Thoreau and Conway walked together on July 9, 1853 (XI, 337).

There is a tradition, recorded by Walter Harding in "Thoreau and the Negro," *Negro History Bulletin,* X (October 1946), 23, that a little statue of Uncle Tom holding Little Eva, now among the Thoreau relics in the Concord Antiquarian Society museum, was given him by a fugitive slave whom he helped get to Canada.

[12] William E. Channing, *Thoreau: the Poet-Naturalist* (Boston, 1873), p. 77.

[13] Wilbur H. Siebert, "The Underground Railroad in Massachusetts," *Proceedings of the American Antiquarian Society,* XLV, Part 1 (April 1935), 36.

To expect more would be to misunderstand Thoreau's position. Although he now recognized that there were increasing numbers of people who could be relied on to find the same political morality in their hearts as he did, he still remained on the fringe of the antislavery movement. The conflict between action and contemplation still lay unresolved within his soul and very likely played its part in the decision, taken toward the end of 1851, to devote a major part of his spare time not to antislavery but to the calendar of the seasons and to other quiet scientific pursuits. And in the field of political action he continued to defend theses which marked him as a sectary. Like the followers of Phillips and Garrison at this time, Thoreau's appeal was still solely from principle, and he excluded voting and running for office from among his acceptable actions. But he set himself apart even from the small coalition that clustered around the *Liberator*. For although it included men and women who were ideologically his nearest of kin, he would not join any of its organizations. He gave his advice about not buying conservative newspapers to all abolitionists as a class, but it is evident that he was still thinking of parallel individual actions and not of action organized and captained.

It is not surprising, therefore, to discover that the sentences which Thoreau composed on the rendition of Sims were spoken only to himself. He apparently intended them for a Concord audience, perhaps the one which gathered on May 3 to hear Emerson on the same subject,[14] and he made much of the ironical coincidence which brought the anniversary of the battles of Concord and Lexington exactly a week after Sims's return to slavery. No one asked him to talk, however, and he wrote in his journal, "It is not the invitation which I hear, but which I feel, that I obey" (VIII, 181). But the invitation was perhaps more important to him than he admitted, for the composition which had begun hopefully remained, so far as can now be determined, a collection of fragments.

II

It was these fragments that became the nucleus of a lecture which Thoreau delivered to an assorted antislavery audience on July 4, 1854,

[14] Ralph L. Rusk, *The Life of Ralph Waldo Emerson* (New York, 1949), p. 367.

in Framingham. In the three years which separated "Carrying Off Sims" from "Slavery in Massachusetts," Thoreau's position on the strategy of abolition did not undergo any significant change.

He omitted from his lecture the statement welcoming a war between North and South on the question of slavery. But his underlying thesis continued to be that in order to bring social realities into correspondence with higher law the common people had to go behind the legal apparatus of the status quo and act in such a way as to create precedents for a new legality. "The law will never make men free," he declared; "it is men who have got to make the law free. They are lovers of law and order who observe the law when the government breaks it" (IV, 396).

At the time he spoke, men were already on trial for having attempted to rescue a fugitive whom the government of Massachusetts had later succeeded in returning to slavery. Some two months earlier, Anthony Burns had been taken in Boston under circumstances much like those of Thomas Sims, and on the night of April 26 a group of men organized by Thomas Wentworth Higginson had almost succeeded in storming the Court House and taking Burns out of the hands of constitutionally established authority.[15] To Higginson and his associates Henry Thoreau gave full support. "My sympathies in this case," he declared, "are wholly with the accused, and wholly against their accusers and judges" (IV, 404).

Still associated, as it had been in 1851, with this advocacy of revolutionary mass action was Thoreau's opposition to the method of politics. He had faith in the introspection of men and women whose hearts led them to the direct attack and apparently recognized the validity of organization for such an end, but he discovered no virtue in either the thinking or association of those who were bounded by legality. The fate of America, he wrote, "does not depend on what kind of paper you drop into the ballot-box once a year, but on what kind of man you drop from your chamber into the street every morning" (IV, 403). Those who limited themselves to voting and the Constitution would obey the devil himself if the majority had elected him, and indeed Thoreau could not persuade himself that he did not al-

---

[15] Channing, *A History of the United States*, VI, 107–9.

ready "dwell *wholly within* hell" (IV, 405). But before he would be party to any such devil-serving arrangement as the American government he would "touch a match to blow up earth and hell together" (IV, 315).

In place of voting, Thoreau once again recommended the tactics of "Civil Disobedience" and "Carrying Off Sims": that every upright man withhold his support from evil governments and evil newspapers. He said nothing specifically now about not paying one's poll tax, and he moved closer to the Garrisonians in his audience by advocating that Massachusetts "dissolve her union with the slaveholder" (IV, 403), but the principle is unmistakable. "Let the judge and the jury, and the sheriff and the jailer, cease to act under a corrupt government,—cease to be tools and become men" (XII, 365)—so he wrote in his journal at this time, and in the lecture itself he suggested that the governor "could at least have *resigned* himself into fame" (IV, 390). Equally with the officials, every citizen of Massachusetts ought to "dissolve his union with her, as long as she delays to do her duty" (IV, 403).

If Thoreau in 1854 had an audience to address at Framingham it was not because of any change in the policies he advocated but because of a change in the nation and therefore among the abolitionists. There is no evidence to corroborate Moncure Conway's statement that he was "now clamoured for."[16] But he did get an invitation to speak, and with printings in both the *Liberator* and Greeley's *Tribune*,[17] his address undoubtedly reached more people than any other work of his had done before. It has been suggested that he was welcomed "as a spokesman for many hitherto aloof intellectuals,"[18] and Conway wrote that Thoreau's importance at the Framingham meeting was as "a representative of Concord, of science and letters, which could not quietly pursue their tasks while slavery was trampling down the rights of mankind."[19] But this view, doubtless correct in small

---

[16] *Autobiography*, I, 184.
[17] *Liberator*, XXIV (July 21, 1854), 116. For the editorial with which Greeley accompanied his printing of the address on August 2, 1854, see the *Thoreau Society Bulletin* for April 1945.
[18] Henry S. Canby, *Thoreau* (Boston, 1939), p. 386.
[19] *Autobiography*, I, 184 f.

part, suffers in both instances from retrospection, for *Walden* had not yet been published and Thoreau's reputation as a writer was then little more than parochial. What is perhaps more to the point is that the Fugitive Slave Law and the Kansas-Nebraska Act had set the nation as a whole, and in the North the abolitionists in particular, on the highroad to the Civil War. The violence already in sight was to be localized—and Thoreau, whose speech showed no interest in the territories, did not receive the invitations for additional readings that he was to get after Harper's Ferry—but the advance toward nation-wide conflict was undoubtedly begun.

An instance of this development among the abolitionists—others can be found elsewhere[20]—is presented in the *Liberator* at the very time of Thoreau's address. In an undated but obviously recent letter to a friend in Massachusetts, Angelina Grimké, wife of Theodore Weld and in her own right a significant antislavery agitator, announces her abandonment of nonresistance and her new conviction that nothing but violence will bring an end to slavery. "It is time," she writes, "that the alarm-bell was rung through the Northern States, and that the holy resolution was solemnly, universally adopted, that, cost what it may, no fugitive from slavery should ever go back from Northern soil." One may argue that "a civil war must be the result of such a course," and so it would, but "if we cannot do our duty to the oppressed millions of our country and the world without war, let it come, both servile and civil; for I now entirely despair of the triumph of Justice and Humanity without shedding of blood. A temporary war," she concludes, "is an incomparably less evil than permanent slavery."[21]

Miss Grimké was still in the minority among the Garrisonians, and her view was repudiated by Garrison himself and by the even more dogmatic pacifist Adin Ballou.[22] But it was a minority that was to grow, and Thoreau was momentarily one of its spokesmen.

---

[20] See especially Herbert Aptheker, "Militant Abolitionism," in his *To Be Free: Studies in American Negro History* (New York, 1948), pp. 41–74.

[21] *Liberator*, XXIV (July 7, 1854), 106.

[22] *Liberator*, XXIV (July 28, 1854), 117.

His suggested boycott of proslavery newspapers received no recorded support; it was his appeal to violent resistance that was bringing him into harmony with the times. But it was a meeting on the narrowest of grounds—a single doctrine when the crisis demanded a broad platform, and mere words, unaccompanied for the most part by the very actions they advocated.

It seems impossible to avoid the conclusion that in relation to slavery in 1854 Thoreau was still chiefly concerned with the internal cleansing of a man who held that reform was first of the soul and only secondarily of the world. Even the violent disobedience he advocated became in the end simply a gesture.

Higginson and the others who had charged the Court House had been in accord with the higher law and therefore their action was just; its immediate success or failure and its ultimate repercussions did not seem to concern him. He had learned to distrust Fame, he wrote, "which considers not the simple heroism of an action, but only as it is connected with its apparent consequences" (IV, 403). Since it was the act itself that counted for Thoreau, and not its results, he expected Higginson to plead guilty and take his punishment (IV, 404), much as he himself had done when Sam Staples demanded his tax. Wendell Phillips, on the contrary, who knew that Higginson would probably be found guilty under American law, advised him to plead innocent and thus "gain a jury in order to argue before them the *higher law*." Phillips, though he agreed with Thoreau at this time in eschewing political parties, was planning for the propaganda that helps build movements, and the attack on the Court House was less a symbol for him than a step in a campaign. "The opportunity of preaching to that jury," he advised Higginson, "is one of the things you fought for, perhaps the most important object."[23]

Henry Thoreau continued to place himself outside of organized movements and presumably above them. "Show me a free state, and a court truly of justice," he declared, "and I will fight for them, if need be" (IV, 404). But he did not say how he would go about cre-

---

[23] Quoted in Oscar Sherwin's unpublished doctoral dissertation, "Prophet of Liberty: A Biography of Wendell Phillips" (New York University, 1940), p. 280.

ating a free state and courts truly of justice. Confronted by the same problem at the same time, Bronson Alcott, who had provided the example which Thoreau followed in refusing to pay his tax and who had long been with Thoreau among the nonvoters, wrote: "I must see to it that my part is done hereafter to give us a Boston, a Mayor, a Governor, and a President . . . so I shall vote, as I have never done hitherto, for a municipal government and a state." He still believed that "something besides voting" would be needed to rescue the nation from slavery, but he was allowing himself preliminary strategies.[24] Alcott, moreover, the one-time nonresistant and no-organizationist, had become a member of the Boston Vigilance Committee during the Sims affair, and in the attempt to free Burns had taken what Higginson considered a heroic part.[25]

Compared with the violent resistance defended and carried out by such men as Phillips and Alcott, Thoreau's is seen to lack body, for he took no part in the movements which alone could make it either unnecessary or successful. But every political coalition needs its radical catalysts, and such a one was Henry Thoreau. A half-dozen years after the frustrated attack on the Boston Court House, when one of Thoreau's tributes to John Brown was being read to abolitionists gathered at the martyr's grave in North Elba, the chairman prefaced his reading with praise for the author, a man "whom all must honor who know him": "Of a fearless, truthful soul, living near to Nature, with ear attuned to catch her simplest and most subtle thought, and heart willing to interpret them to his willing brain, he often speaks undisguised, in most nervous Saxon, the judgment upon great events which others, either timid or powerless of speech, so long to hear expressed."[26] The "often" was an exaggeration, but the assessment of Thoreau was just. The absolutism of his belief in obedience to higher law fitted him to call attention to those issues on which ultimately no compromise was possible and no resting with persuasion and ballots. His own struggle with quietism, moreover, which prevented his acting out the militancy he so much admired,

---

[24] *The Journals of Bronson Alcott*, p. 273.

[25] *Ibid.*, pp. 244, 272, 445 f.

[26] *Liberator*, XXX (July 27, 1860), 117.

gave his words a force aroused by no other subject. What he later said of John Brown might as well have been said of himself, that he was "a volcano with an ordinary chimney-flue" (IV, 413). His speeches on slavery paid the debt which one aspect of his personality owed the other. Their intensity came from the pent conflict within.

III

The triumph of Thoreau's narrow vein of radicalism was in his defense of John Brown. His doctrine had not changed since the attempt to free Anthony Burns, but circumstances had: the genteel and romantically military Higginson had been succeeded by the single-minded and overpoweringly heroic Captain Brown, and the anti-slavery North had unknowingly reached the threshold beyond which it could hail such a man and such an unswerving morality.

Thoreau's "Plea for Captain John Brown" is still, on the level of doctrine, the statement of a thinker who is outside parties and organizations and who has no grasp of the impulses that govern politics in men built differently from himself. He no longer speaks of boycotting conservative newspapers, the day for so timid a blow having presumably passed. But he is still a disunionist, taking exception to Brown's "respect for the Constitution and his faith in the permanence" of the union between the states (IV, 411), he still derides politics, and he still measures political acts only with the ruler of principle, careless of consequences.

The contrast between the method of politicians and the method of John Brown provides an obverse of contempt to the coin whose brighter side is idealization of the hero. Brown was one of the Puritans, declares Thoreau, who were "neither Democrats nor Republicans, but men of simple habits, straightforward, prayerful, not thinking much of rulers who did not fear God, not making many compromises, nor seeking after available candidates" (IV, 412). And later, commenting on one newspaper's abridgment of Brown's words to make room for the proceedings of a convention: "To turn from the voices and deeds of earnest men to the *cackling* of political conventions! Office-seekers and speech-makers, who do not so much as lay an honest egg, but wear their breasts bare upon an egg of chalk! Their great game is the game of straws, or rather that universal aboriginal game of the platter, at which the Indians cried *hub bub!*" (IV, 421 f.)

Tucked away in the address is the statement that Brown ought not to be hanged and the suggestion that all who oppose his execution "say so distinctly" (IV, 437). But for the most part, as he confesses himself (IV, 425), Thoreau speaks of Brown as already dead and appears before America not to plead "for his life, but for his character,—his immortal life" (IV, 438). Here, as in 1854, there is no interest in practical success or failure but only in that illustration of the higher law which Thoreau had believed in from the beginning. The hero, like the brave man of "The Service," by being right himself, will induce rightness in others. Those who do not understand Brown "do not know that like the seed is the fruit, and that, in the moral world, when good seed is planted, good fruit is inevitable, and does not depend on our watering and cultivating; that when you plant, or bury, a hero in his field, a crop of heroes is sure to spring up" (IV, 418). Divorced as before from movements and effects, he speaks only from his own preconceptions and from his estimate of the individual.

The two occasions on which Thoreau met Brown, one early in 1857, the other shortly before the march to Harper's Ferry,[27] were

---

[27] Thoreau distinguished between the two meetings in "A Plea for Captain John Brown," referring to Brown's being in Concord "some years ago" and to "his speech here" (IV, 413), but the printed journals contain no sentences about Brown dated at the time of either visit and no references to missing pages that might have been torn out of the manuscript books for use in the lectures composed at the end of 1859 and the beginning of 1860. The first visit was in 1857, but the two primary sources of information do not agree on the month. F. B. Sanborn, *Recollections of Seventy Years* (2 vols.; Boston, 1909), says it was in March (I, 102) and provides several paragraphs of details (I, 102–4, 110). The *Journals of Ralph Waldo Emerson* give the month as February (IX, 81). Allan Nevins, *The Emergence of Lincoln* (2 vols.; New York and London, 1950), writes that in the opinion of the John Brown collector Boyd B. Stutler this visit took place about February 18, but he does not describe the evidence on which Mr. Stutler bases this conclusion (II, 12 n.). Sanborn's *Recollections* give May 7, 1859, as the date of Brown's arrival in Concord for the second visit (I, 163), and this is corroborated by *The Journals of Bronson Alcott*, which record Thoreau's presence at the lecture given by Brown at the Concord Town Hall on May 8 (p. 315).

enough to convince him that here was the hero he had long ago projected. John Brown satisfied Thoreau's demand for a man with a
higher aim in life than longevity or acquisition. He seemed to be "a
transcendentalist above all, a man of ideas and principles, . . . not
yielding to a whim or transient impulse, but carrying out the purpose
of a life" (IV, 413). This purpose, moreover, he believed to derive
from the godhead, and while his metaphysics was more conventional
than Thoreau's, he manifestly shared the transcendentalist's belief in
direct perception of the higher law. Unlike the convention-bound
majority, whose defects of soul led them to worship one or another
sort of idol, Brown "did not set up even a political graven image
between him and his God" (IV, 419).

But what undoubtedly weighed most with Thoreau was the presence of these traits in a soldier. He had no use for the discipline of
obedience in the relation between wage-serving private and officer,
and he could witness in himself the limitations of principle in a man
who was not "continuously inspired" to its execution (IV, 433). In
John Brown he found ideals wedded to discipline, the hero who willed
to execute the higher law not on occasion but day by day. It was
Captain John Brown whom he celebrated, the man who, nearing
sixty, must still "eat sparingly and fare hard, as became a soldier"
(IV, 413), the militant who strode directly to the goal even in his
speech, the reformer whose distinguishing mark was "that the tyrant
must give place to him or he to the tyrant" (IV, 433).

It is this image of the man of principle in elemental direct struggle
with evil that informs Thoreau's incisive sentences. Brown's "company was small indeed," he writes, "because few could be found
worthy to pass muster. Each one who there laid down his life for the
poor and oppressed was a picked man, culled out of many thousands,
if not millions; apparently a man of principle, of rare courage, and
devoted humanity; ready to sacrifice his life at any moment for the
benefit of his fellow-man. . . . These alone were ready to step between the oppressor and the oppressed" (IV, 432). True, they used
methods not generally countenanced. But "the question is not about
the weapon, but the spirit in which you use it" (IV, 434). "The slave-
ship is on her way, crowded with its dying victims; new cargoes are
being added in mid-ocean; a small crew of slaveholders, countenanced

by a large body of passengers, is smothering four millions under the hatches, and yet the politician asserts that the only proper way by which deliverance is to be obtained is by 'the quiet diffusion of the sentiments of humanity,' without any 'outbreak.' As if the sentiments of humanity were ever found unaccompanied by its deeds, and you could disperse them, all finished to order, the pure article, as easily as water with a watering-pot, and so lay the dust. What is that that I hear cast overboard? The bodies of the dead that have found deliverance. That is the way we are 'diffusing' humanity, and its sentiments with it" (IV, 423 f.). "I think," he declares, "that for once the Sharp's rifles and the revolvers were employed in a righteous cause" (IV, 434).

Given Thoreau's preconceptions and given his expectations gratified in the two meetings with Brown and in the reports from Virginia, it is not difficult to understand why he should have been among the very first to speak out in the man's favor. Unlike those more deeply involved in political conflict, Thoreau did not have to pause and evaluate the effects of Harper's Ferry and of his own sympathies. His sole task was to call attention to the greatness of the deed performed. On his own initiative, therefore, and disregarding the warnings of Republicans, of Garrisonians, and even of Frank Sanborn, who had been one of Brown's associates, he sent notices about Concord announcing his address.[28]

If once again, as in 1854, he gathered hearers, it was not because of any change in the policies he advocated, but once more because of a change in the nation. "Years were not required for a revolution of public opinion," he himself wrote shortly afterward; "days, nay hours, produced marked changes in this case" (IV, 442). Once before he had been a minor spokesman for the militant wing of abolitionism. Now the movement of which Brown had quickly become the symbol shouldered its mass forward to the direct assault and invited him to strive for a more significant role.

The day after the execution of the martyr, Thoreau was asked by Frank Sanborn to take Emerson's horse and covered wagon and escort

---

[28] Canby, *Thoreau*, p. 391; Ralph Waldo Emerson, "Biographical Sketch" of Thoreau in the latter's *Writings*, I, xx.

a Mr. Lockwood to the railroad station at South Acton and there put him on the first train to Canada. Thoreau asked no questions and went about the business. Lockwood was Frank Meriam, one of two who who had escaped from Harper's Ferry. Thoreau did not know his identity at the time, but he knew enough to call him "X" in the journal and to be firm about getting him out of the country. Meriam had been unsettled by the shock of his recent experiences, was concerned about Fate and very likely his soul as well, and wanted to consult Emerson. After he learned that his unidentified escort was not Emerson, he jumped out of the wagon to run back to Concord. "How Thoreau got him in again," writes Sanborn, "he never told me; but I suspected some judicious use of force, accompanying the grave persuasive speech natural to our friend" (XIX, 3f.; VI, 366f.).

Some three months later he again helped defend a member of John Brown's group, this time Sanborn himself. In February of 1860, Sanborn had fled to Canada after being voted in contempt of the Senate for refusing to testify at a Washington hearing on Harper's Ferry. Early in April, when he had returned to Concord and thought himself safe, he was disturbed in his home one evening by the intrusion of four men who arrested him on order of the Senate and proceeded to drag him out to their carriage. While Sanborn resisted with squirming body and kicking feet, his sister shouted to the neighbors, and the antislavery people of Concord rushed out to foil the arrest. They succeeded in holding the agents off long enough for the local judge to write out a writ of habeas corpus, and Sanborn was then committed to house arrest—but allowed a pistol in case he again needed to defend himself. The next day he was taken to Boston, where Chief Justice Shaw ordered him released.[29] That same day Thoreau wrote in his journal, "Lodged at Sanborn's last night after his *rescue,* he being away" (XIX, 241).

But although he was thus willing to aid Brown's immediate followers in Concord, where the problem brought itself to him much as the fugitive slaves had arrived in his family's home, he was unwilling to take the steps that would have placed him more firmly and significantly among the people whom he had helped and spoken for.

---

[29] Sanborn, *Recollections of Seventy Years,* I, 208–17.

Sanborn reports that Mrs. George L. Stearns, wife of one of Brown's important supporters, asked him to write a biography of John Brown, but that Thoreau refused, "because he had his own manuscripts to edit, and specially those relating to the red man."[30]

In a parallel fashion, Thoreau accepted two invitations to speak on John Brown but backed away when it seemed he might be drawn further into the abolitionist movement. He had delivered "A Plea for Captain John Brown" on his own initiative in Concord on the thirtieth of October. The next day a telegram arrived in Concord asking him to lecture before Theodore Parker's congregation in Boston on the first of November.[31] Parker was in Europe, on the trip which he never came back from, and the scheduled speaker at his church was Frederick Douglass. But Douglass, though he had not approved of Brown's plans, had been, like Parker, his known associate, and had recently fled from Philadelphia only a few hours before he was to have been arrested.[32] The substitution of Thoreau proved to be a success. "A very large audience listened to this lecture," wrote the reporter for the *Liberator,* "crowding the hall half an hour before the time of its commencement, and giving hearty applause to some of the most energetic expressions of the speaker."[33]

Thoreau's second invitation to speak came at his own request. The day after he lectured in Concord, he wrote to his friend Blake in Worcester offering to repeat his talk without any fee save expenses (VI, 358). Arrangements were quickly made, and Thoreau lectured in that town on the third of November.[34] Whether he was as successful as in Boston is not known, but circumstances were in his favor,

---

[30] F. B. Sanborn, ed., *The First and Last Journeys of Thoreau* (2 vols.; Boston, 1905), I, xxxvi.

[31] Charles W. Slack to H. D. Thoreau or R. W. Emerson, a telegram among Thoreau's "Miscellaneous Holograph Notes" in the Henry W. and Albert A. Berg Collection of the New York Public Library, by whose permission it is here mentioned.

[32] Philip S. Foner, ed., *The Life and Writings of Frederick Douglass* (4 vols.; New York, 1950–55), II, 90–92.

[33] *Liberator,* XXIX (November 4, 1859), 174.

[34] Ruth H. Frost, "Thoreau's Worcester Visits," *Nature Outlook,* I (February 1943), 14.

for Worcester was the home of Thomas Wentworth Higginson, and in the letter to Blake Thoreau had suggested that "perhaps Higginson may like to have a meeting." So firm were its militant abolitionists that a few days later, looking about for men to rescue those who might be arrested in connection with Harper's Ferry, Sanborn wrote Higginson that while such a rescue would "do very well in Worcester" it would be "rather precarious in Boston," and asked whether his "Worcester people [would] go down to Boston to take Dr. Howe or Wendell Phillips out of the marshal's hands."[35]

After reading his lecture twice to sympathetic audiences, Thoreau refused to go further. In the summer of 1860, Parker's society (its leader now dead) invited Thoreau to address its annual picnic at Waverly, a few miles from home, and the abolitionists asked him to speak at a memorial meeting near John Brown's grave in North Elba, New York. "Of course," he wrote to his sister, "I did not go to North Elba, but I sent some reminiscences of last fall," and "I do not go to picnics, even in Concord, you know" (VI, 363 f.).

Thoreau's extremist position, we have suggested, allowed him to serve as a catalyst for others, pointing out to them a goal they must in time be forced to attain and thereby helping them move forward to positions not quite so far along the road. But since he withdrew from involvement with the people he acted upon, he could only teach them and not, as he needed, learn from them. He does not seem to have grasped the depth and breadth of the transformation then occurring in the land, and could see in the North's unwilling admiration for Brown only "the possibility, in the course of ages, of a revolution in behalf of another and an oppressed people" (IV, 443), carried out by men awakened to the higher law. But that revolution not having appeared, he returned to the examination of nature.

IV

Had the abolition of slavery waited upon an adequate increase in the number of men and women willing to undertake it from principle, it might very well not have come any sooner than Thoreau expected.

---

[35] Sanborn, *Recollections of Seventy Years,* I, 205.

But he lived to see the outbreak of a civil war incorporating the war for freedom which he had been ready to welcome ten years earlier and had one more invitation to modify his attitude toward ballots and toward political organization.

The definition of Thoreau's attitude to the Civil War is made difficult by a serious lack of evidence. He had fallen ill early in December of 1860, and in what was left of the winter fought a painfully quiet campaign with tuberculosis. The forces which had driven on his intense research in forestry, so mighty as to cut off the usual miscellany of his earlier observation, were suddenly quieted. He was confined to the house, his study of nature reduced to the reports and specimens brought home by young Horace Mann and to whatever he could make of Channing's well-meant inaccuracies. He mustered enough energy to undertake surveying jobs for two of his oldest customers on the first and second of January.[36] Then he was back in his room. Not till the seventh of April, after emerging gradually and at intervals, was he able to walk two miles (XX, 335). His old physical resources were no longer available. When Fort Sumter was fired upon a few days later, plans were already being made to send him on a trip to Minnesota in search of health.

During this period, and for the months remaining, Thoreau wrote a mere handful of letters. His journal, swollen by great labor in the two years preceding, dwindled first to an occasional short paragraph and then to nothing. He was a practical man and a writer, and when he realized that his life was ending he did not undertake new compositions but gave what energy he had to polishing lectures already completed.

He did, indeed, see a number of his old friends and a few newer ones, and when the letters and diaries and jottings of all these people are located and combed through they will perhaps reveal more of what was going on in his mind. But what is available today is disappointingly bare. Thus Ricketson visited Thoreau in August and September of 1861, but the extracts so far printed from his journal reveal very little of their conversations.[37] Similarly the letters which Horace

---

[36] "Field Notes of Surveys," pp. 123, 141.

[37] Anna and Walton Ricketson, eds., *Daniel Ricketson and his Friends* (New Bedford, 1902), pp. 302 f., 317–19.

Mann sent home while accompanying Thoreau to Minnesota mention the war only once, and then to say that there is little news of it.[38]

There is enough evidence, however, to show that while these last two years brought a significant step in Thoreau's support of the Union, they did not change his underlying attitude toward social action.

The direct assault on slavery which he had praised in John Brown as an individual he now welcomed in the government and the nation. Sanborn writes that Thoreau believed "from the beginning that it would prove a war for emancipation, which he foresaw and predicted."[39] Similarly Conway reports that even after the defeat at Bull Run, Thoreau was "in a state of exultation about the moral regeneration of the nation."[40] Like the Garrisonians as a group, he now forgot the old belief in the proslavery character of the Constitution and the old strategy of disunion[41] and regained the country he had earlier lost. In defense of the Union he was "as zealous as any soldier," writes Sanborn (VI, 392); and Henry Salt preserves the tradition that Thoreau used to say he could "never recover while the war lasted," that when the victory of freedom seemed in doubt he was "sick for his country."[42]

In "Slavery in Massachusetts," as has been noted, he had said, "Show me a free state and a court truly of justice, and I will fight for them, if need be" (IV, 404), and in "The Last Days of John Brown" he had spoken of "a revolution in behalf of another and an oppressed people" (IV, 443). The Civil War had none of this purity of intention that Thoreau wished for, and it seems likely that with Wendell Phillips and other radical abolitionists[43] Thoreau believed it necessary to

---

[38] Letter to the writer from the present owner of the letters, Mr. Robert L. Straker, August 29, 1955.

[39] *The Life of Henry David Thoreau* (Boston and New York, 1917), p. 401.

[40] *Autobiography*, I, 335.

[41] Russell B. Nye, *William Lloyd Garrison and the Humanitarian Reformers* (Boston and Toronto, 1955), p. 169 f.

[42] Henry S. Salt, *Life of Henry David Thoreau* (London, 1896), p. 143 f.

[43] Nye, p. 176.

prod the government to submerge lesser interests and make the war truly one that would permanently free the slaves. Thus in December of 1861, Alcott reports that Thoreau "does not conceal his impatience with the slowness of the present administration and its disregard of honor and justice to the free sentiments of the North." And a month later he again records Thoreau's impatience with "what he calls the temporizing policy of our rulers."[44]

Thoreau thus attained during the Civil War a position in regard to slavery which paralleled his position in regard to agriculture and industry. The enforcement of the higher law on the question of freedom was in the hands of the federal government. There, however, it was necessarily mixed with lesser motives. How was the interested citizen to make certain that the government would act in accordance with principle?

As late as the end of 1860, Thoreau had told Alcott that he still did not think it proper to vote for President.[45] But earlier that same year, congratulating Charles Sumner on an antislavery speech in the Senate, he wrote: "I wish to thank you for your speech on the Barbarism of Slavery, which, I hope and suspect, commences a new era in the history of our Congress; when questions of national importance have come to be considered occasionally from a broadly ethical, and not from a narrowly political point of view." It was refreshing to him to hear "naked truth" in Congress, where it had "only been employed occasionally to perfume the wheel-grease of party or national politics." Not only did he praise Sumner, but Gerrit Smith as well, who had been elected by antislavery forces at a time when Thoreau would have nothing to do with politics. Gerrit Smith's "whole value" in Congress, it now seemed to Thoreau, six years after Smith had resigned his seat, had been as a speaker of such naked truth, truth "which can always take care of itself when uttered and of course belongs to no party."[46]

---

[44] *The Journals of Bronson Alcott,* pp. 341, 343.

[45] *Ibid.,* p. 330.

[46] Thoreau to Sumner, July 16, 1860, ms. in the Harvard University Library. Part of this letter is printed in *The Works of Charles Sumner* (15 vols.; Boston, 1872), V, 169 f.

Here indeed is a hint that even as Thoreau had found a government just enough to merit his support in war, so he might have found a legislature worth electing just men to. But there is no evidence that he did so.

V

Thoreau's social thinking thus ends on a fruitful inconsistency. In each of its three chief areas it arrives at the recognition that the achievement of correspondence with higher law is not a matter solely for the individual but for society as well. Beyond this recognition lies organized political action, whose threshold Henry Thoreau never crosses. But it is only by crossing it that the pressure of the inconsistency can be relieved.

What Thoreau would have done had he lived is beyond conjecture. Recollecting what has been said of his personality, however, we can understand why his development was so hesitant, why he was outdistanced in the matter of politics and organizations by men like Alcott and Phillips.

His social thought is transitional. The America in which he began to think and to act—the two never separated for him—was still a new land, in which the geographical opening to the West seemed to correspond to a social opening toward ideal commonwealths and perfect men. The nation fully born shortly after he died could look forward to a long period of stability, during which the betterment of mankind would come only step by step and with great labor. It was to be a time for hacking at the branches of evil, not striking at the root. The germ of Thoreau's response to this modern America has already been exposed in his suggestions for legislative and military acts to limit the acquisition of individuals in favor of the life and spiritual growth of the people. But the passage from the earlier period to the later could not be completed without solving another problem.

The Thoreau who had returned to Concord and accepted the world could no longer consistently think, as did the man who moved out to the pond, of the single individual reforming and revolutionizing himself to attain spherical correspondence with the oversoul and thereby helping to perfect the world. The simple life and the true use of nature had now to be reached within and by means of the social order, and the joint perfection of men and society required a new solution of Thoreau's old problem: the conflict between quietism and militancy, between contemplation and action.

He had glimpsed one answer in the man of the John Brown type, who "did not wait till he was personally interfered with or thwarted in some harmless business before he gave his life to the cause of the oppressed." But he himself was only in one aspect such a person. All through the period of which we have been writing, most of Thoreau's hours were given over to the "harmless business" of mastering nature and language. And when great crises dramatized in individual heroism touched him, his normally premeditated activity was hurried and tugged at by conflicting impulses as the opposing elements of his personality fought out their ideological differences.

When the battle reports from Kansas had challenged him beyond endurance, he went desperately out of the house one afternoon determined to find and taste a certain cranberry. But it was not just nature he ran out to. He joined the cranberry to his old idea of reform. His job was not to attack the evil outside him but to wash his hands of it, purify himself, and turn his face toward perfection: "For only absorbing employment prevails, succeeds, takes up space, occupies territory, determines the future of individuals and states, drives Kansas out of your head, and actually and permanently occupies the only desirable and free Kansas against all border ruffians. The attitude of resistance is one of weakness, inasmuch as it only faces an enemy; it has its back to all that is truly attractive" (XV, 36).

The outcome of this conflict was not, as we have seen, always the same. Nature requires serenity, and who could be serene when Thomas Sims and Anthony Burns had been returned to slavery or when John Brown was waiting to be hanged? But the pendulum always swung back. When "The Last Days of John Brown" was being read for him at North Elba, Thoreau was studying the rate of growth of white pine and observing the waving uncut grass on a neighbor's land. "It is a beautiful Camilla," he wrote, "sweeping like waves of light and shade over the whole breadth of his land, like a low steam curling over it, imparting wonderful life to the landscape, like the light and shade of a changeable garment, waves of light and shade pursuing each other over the whole breadth of the landscape like waves hastening to break on a shore" (XIX, 385).

The conflicting impulses toward and away from direct action persist into the war itself. Writing to the abolitionist Parker Pillsbury on April 10, 1861, at a time when his normal conflict was perhaps aggravated by his illness, he restated his philosophy of reform in much the same terms that he had used twenty years earlier in the essay on Persius. Pillsbury had asked to buy copies of his books for a friend, and Thoreau wrote: "As for your friend, my prospective reader, I hope he ignores Fort Sumter, and 'Old Abe,' and all that; for that is just the most fatal, and, indeed, the only fatal weapon you can direct against evil, ever; for, as long as you *know of it,* you are *particeps criminis.*" But what he wished for his reader he was not able to attain for himself. "Alas!" he exclaims, "*I* have heard of Sumter and Pickens, and even of Buchanan," "I also read the New York Tribune," and adds as if fully aware of his inner workings, "but then I am reading Herodotus and Strabo and Blodget's 'Climatology' and 'Six Years in the Desert of North America,' as hard as I can, to counterbalance it" (VI, 378 f.).

Brown and Thoreau, wrote Alcott at the end of 1859, shared "sturdy manliness, straight-forwardness, and independence," but Brown took "more to the human side" and drove "straight at institutions" while Thoreau contented himself with "railing at them and letting them otherwise alone."[47] Thoreau is not to be condemned for being unable to follow the example of John Brown. There are other personalities than Brown's and therefore other solutions to the problem of the individual's perfection through his relation to society. His failure to discover his own solution may be responsible, as much as his early death, for the incompleteness one senses about his career. But perhaps we are mistaken in asking completion and should rather be satisfied with growth. In our earlier discussion of the essay "Walking," we pointed out that in the utopian aspect of his later years Thoreau responded to this manifesto of the conquest of frontiers by trying to discover in imagination the life that he had failed to establish at the pond. Now that the evolution of his realistic aspect has been

---

[47] *The Journals of Bronson Alcott*, p. 321.

unfolded, we can see that his greater response was in seeking for ways by which the ideals of the Walden experiment might be attained in the industrial society it had been opposed to. His search led in directions he could hardly have anticipated. It brought him before a door that opened not only to political action but also to the questioning of private property. And if we may judge by the heat in which he at moments withdrew from it, he did not give up the security of old ideas without pain. But he continued to live by the transcendentalist principle of growth. "I would fain be assured," he wrote in "Walking," "that I am growing apace and rankly, though my very growth disturb this dull equanimity,—though it be with struggle through long, dark, muggy nights or seasons of gloom."

Works Cited

WORKS BY HENRY DAVID THOREAU

The Writings of Henry David Thoreau. 20 vols. Boston and New York, Houghton Mifflin, 1906. This edition, put out by various hands at various times and now in part outdated, includes journals (Vols. VII–XX), correspondence (Vol. VI), poems (Vol. V), Thoreau's only books: *A Week on the Concord and Merrimack Rivers* (Vol. I) and *Walden* (Vol. II), and most of his completed essays. Of the last I have cited most frequently those on Maine (Vol. III), the antislavery essays (Vol. VI), "Life Without Principle" (Vol. IV), "The Succession of Forest Trees" (Vol. V), and "Walking," "Autumnal Tints," and "Wild Apples" (all in Vol. V). "Night and Moonlight," a version of which is in Volume V, was supplemented by *The Moon*. Works not included in this edition are listed below.

"Aulus Persius Flaccus," *Dial,* I (July 1840), 117–21.

"The Correspondence of Henry David Thoreau, 1836–1849." Edited by Walter Harding. Unpublished doctoral dissertation, Rutgers University, 1950.

"Field Notes of Surveys Made by Henry D. Thoreau Since November, 1849." Manuscript notebook in the Concord Free Public Library.

"Henry David Thoreau: the College Essays." Edited by Edwin I. Moser. Unpublished master's thesis, New York University, 1951.

"Homer, Ossian, Chaucer," *Dial,* IV (January 1844), 290–305.

"[Lecture on the Reformer and the Conservative.]" Unpublished manuscript in the Houghton Library of Harvard University.

The Moon. Boston and New York, Houghton Mifflin, 1927. Another version, "Night and Moonlight," appears in *The Writings of Henry David Thoreau,* Volume V.

"Notes on Fruits." Manuscript in the Henry W. and Albert A. Berg Collection of the New York Public Library.

"Notes on Fruits: Four Pages Holograph." Manuscript in the Henry W. and Albert A. Berg Collection of the New York Public Library.

"Order of Flowers Accidentally Observed in '51." Manuscript in the Henry E. Huntington Library.

"[Portion of Holograph Journal, 1860–1861.]" Manuscript in the Henry W. and Albert A. Berg Collection of the New York Public Library.

The Service. Edited by F. B. Sanborn. Boston, Charles E. Goodspeed, 1902.

OTHER WORKS

Adams, Raymond. "The Bibliographical History of Thoreau's *A Week on the Concord and Merrimack Rivers,*" *Papers of the Bibliographical Society of America,* XLIII (First Quarter, 1949), 39–47.

Adams, Robert. "Nathaniel Peabody Rogers: 1794–1846," *New England Quarterly,* XX (September 1947), 365–76.

Aptheker, Herbert. To Be Free: Studies in American Negro History. New York, International, 1948.

Austin, George L. The Life and Times of Wendell Phillips. Boston, Lee and Shepard, 1884.

Ballou, Adin. A Discourse on the Subject of American Slavery, Delivered in the First Congregational Meeting House, in Mendon, Mass., July 4, 1837. Boston, Isaac Knapp, 1837.

Belknap, Jeremy. The History of New Hampshire. 3 vols. Dover, New Hampshire, Crosby and Varney, 1821.

Bode, Carl. "Thoreau and His Last Publishers," *New England Quarterly,* XXVI (September 1953), 383–87.

Broderick, John G. "Imagery in *Walden,*" *University of Texas Studies in English,* XXXIII (1954), 80–89.

Burtis, Mary E. Moncure Conway, 1832–1907. New Brunswick, New Jersey, Rutgers University Press, 1952.

Canby, Henry S. Thoreau. Boston and New York, Houghton Mifflin, 1939.

Carmer, Carl. The Hudson. New York and Toronto, Farrar and Rinehart, 1939.

Channing, Edward. A History of the United States. 6 vols. New York, Macmillan, 1926.

Channing, William Ellery (1780–1842). The Works of William E. Channing, D.D. Boston, American Unitarian Association, 1875.

Channing, William Ellery (1810–84). Thoreau: the Poet-Naturalist. Boston, Roberts Brothers, 1873.

Conway, Moncure D. Autobiography: Memoirs and Experiences. 2 vols. Boston and New York, Houghton Mifflin, 1904.

———. "Thoreau," *Fraser's Magazine,* LXXIII (April 1866), 447–65.

Cook, Reginald L. The Concord Saunterer. Middlebury, Vermont, Middlebury College Press, 1940.

Cosman, Max. "Thoreau Faced War," *Personalist,* XXV (January 1944), 73–76.

Coxe, Tench. A View of the United States of America. Philadelphia, William Hall and Wrigley & Berriman, 1794.

"Cultivating Forests," in *Report of the Commissioner of Patents for the Year 1851. Part 2: Agriculture.* Washington, Government Printing Office, 1852.

Davis, Charles H. Life of Charles Henry Davis, Rear Admiral, 1807–1877. Boston and New York, Houghton Mifflin, 1899.

Davis, Charles Henry. " 'The Coast Survey of the United States': A Reply to an Article, with the Above Title, in the February Number of the Merchants' Magazine," *Hunt's Merchants' Magazine,* XX (April 1849), 402–14.

———. "A Memoir Upon the Geological Action of the Tidal and Other Currents of the Ocean," *Memoirs of the American Academy of Arts and Sciences,* New Series, IV, Part 1 (1849), 117–56.

Deevey, Edward S., Jr. "A Re-examination of Thoreau's *Walden,*" *Quarterly Journal of Biology,* XVII (March 1942), 1–11.

Doell, Charles E., and Gerald B. Fitzgerald. A Brief History of Parks and Recreation in the United States. Chicago, Athletic Institute, 1954.

Downing, Andrew J. Cottage Residences; or, A Series of Designs for Rural Cottages and Cottage Villas, and Their Gardens and Grounds, Adapted to North America. 4th ed. New York, John Wiley, 1853.

———. Landscape Gardening. Revised by Frank A. Waugh. 10th ed. New York, John Wiley & Sons, 1921.

———. "The New-York Park," *Horticulturist,* VI (August 1851), 345–49.

———. "On the Improvement of Country Villages," *Horticulturist,* III (June 1849), 545–49.

———. "Our Country Villages," *Horticulturist,* IV (June 1850), 537–41.

———. "Public Cemeteries and Public Gardens," *Horticulturist,* IV (July 1849), 9–12.

Dwight, Timothy. Travels in New-England and New-York. 4 vols. London, William Baynes, 1823.

Emerson, Edward W. Henry Thoreau as Remembered by a Young Friend. Boston and New York, Houghton Mifflin, 1917.

Emerson, Edward W., and Waldo E. Forbes, eds. Journals of Ralph Waldo Emerson. 10 vols. Boston and New York, Houghton Mifflin, 1909–14.

Emerson, George B. A Report on the Trees and Shrubs Growing Naturally in the Forests of Massachusetts. Published Agreeably to an Order of the Legislature by the Commissioners on the Zoological and Botanical Survey of the State. Boston, Dutton and Wentworth, 1846.

Fernhow, Bernhard E. A Brief History of Forestry in the United States and Other Countries. Toronto, University Press, 1907.

Flagg, Wilson. The Woods and By-Ways of New England. Boston, James R. Osgood, 1872.

Foner, Philip S., ed. The Life and Writings of Frederick Douglass. 4 vols. New York, International, 1950–55.

Frost, Ruth H. "Thoreau's Worcester Visits," *Nature Outlook,* I (February 1943), 9–15.

Garrison, Wendell P., and Francis J. Garrison. William Lloyd Garrison, 1805–1879: The Story of His Life Told by His Children. 4 vols. New York, Century, 1885–89.

Glick, Wendell P. "Thoreau and the 'Herald of Freedom,'" *New England Quarterly,* XXII (June 1949), 193–204.

Gordan, John D. "A Thoreau Handbill," *Bulletin of the New York Public Library,* LIX (May 1955), 253–58.

Greeley, Horace. Hints Toward Reforms. 2d ed. New York, Fowler and Wells, 1854.

Harding, Walter. "A Check List of Thoreau's Lectures," *Bulletin of the New York Public Library,* LIII (February 1949), 78–87.

———. "Franklin B. Sanborn and Thoreau's Letters," *Boston Public Library Bulletin,* III (October 1951), 288–93.

———. "Thoreau and the Negro," *Negro History Bulletin,* X (October 1946), 12, 22–23.

Harding, Walter, and Carl Bode. "Henry David Thoreau: A Check

List of His Correspondence," *Bulletin of the New York Public Library*, LIX (May 1955), 227–52.

Hawley, Ralph C. The Practice of Silviculture. 5th ed. New York, John Wiley & Sons, 1946.

Hedge, Frederic Henry. "The Art of Life—the Scholar's Calling," *Dial*, I (October 1840), 175–82.

Hinds, William A. American Communities and Co-operative Colonies. Chicago, Charles H. Kerr, 1908.

Hoeltje, Hubert H. "Thoreau in Concord Church and Town Records," *New England Quarterly*, XII (June 1939), 349–59.

Kittredge, Joseph. Forest Influences: the Effects of Woody Vegetation on Climate, Water, and Soil, with Applications to the Conservation of Water and the Control of Erosion. New York, Toronto, and London, McGraw-Hill, 1948.

Korngold, Ralph. Two Friends of Man: the Story of William Lloyd Garrison and Wendell Phillips and Their Relationship with Abraham Lincoln. Boston, Little, Brown, 1950.

Levy, Leonard W. "Sims' Case: the Fugitive Slave Law in Boston in 1851," *Journal of Negro History*, XXXV (January 1950), 39–74.

Lorch, Fred W. "Thoreau and the Organic Principle in Poetry," *PMLA*, LIII (March 1938), 286–302.

Marsh, George P. The Earth as Modified by Human Action: A New Edition of Man and Nature. New York, Charles Scribner's Sons, 1882.

Masquerier, Lewis. Sociology. New York, published by the author, 1877.

Nevins, Allan. The Emergence of Lincoln. 2 vols. New York, Charles Scribner's Sons, 1950.

———. The Evening Post: A Century of Journalism. New York, Boni and Liveright, 1922.

Noyes, John H. "Perfectionism Not Pro-Slavery," *Perfectionist*, III (October 1, 1843), 61–62.

Nye, Russel B. William Lloyd Garrison and the Humanitarian Reformers. The Library of American Biography, edited by Oscar Handlin. Toronto and Boston, Little, Brown, 1955.

Oehser, Paul H. "Pioneers in Conservation: Footnote to the History of an Idea," *Nature Magazine*, XXXVIII (April 1945), 188–90.

Ogg, Frederic A. National Progress, 1907–1917. Vol. 27 of The American Nation: A History. New York and London, Harper & Bros., 1918.

Parrington, Vernon L. Main Currents in American Thought. 3 vols. in 1. New York, Harcourt, Brace, n.d.

Paul, Sherman. "The Wise Silence: Sound as the Agency of Correspondence in Thoreau," *New England Quarterly,* XXII (December 1949), 511–27.

Phillips, Wendell. "Sketch of . . . Remarks . . . at the Faneuil Hall Bazaar, December 29, 1846," *Liberator,* XVII (January 8, 1847), 7.

Pinchot, Gifford. Breaking New Ground. New York, Harcourt Brace, 1947.

———. "How Conservation Began in the United States," *Agricultural History,* XI (October 1937), 255–65.

Ricketson, Anna, and Walton Ricketson, eds. Daniel Ricketson and His Friends. Boston and New York, Houghton Mifflin, 1902.

———. Daniel Ricketson: Autobiographic and Miscellaneous. New Bedford, Massachusetts, E. Anthony & Sons, 1910.

Rogers, Nathaniel P. A Collection from the Newspaper Writings of Nathaniel Peabody Rogers. Concord, New Hampshire, John R. French, 1847.

Rusk, Ralph L. The Life of Ralph Waldo Emerson. New York, Scribner's, 1949.

Rusk, Ralph L., ed. The Letters of Ralph Waldo Emerson. 6 vols. New York, Columbia University Press, 1939.

Salt, Henry S. Life of Henry David Thoreau. London, Walter Scott, 1896.

Sanborn, Franklin B. Henry D. Thoreau. Boston, Houghton Mifflin, 1882.

———. The Life of Henry David Thoreau. Boston and New York, Houghton Mifflin, 1917.

———. Recollections of Seventy Years. 2 vols. Boston, Richard G. Badger, 1909.

Sanborn, Franklin B., ed. The First and Last Journeys of Thoreau. 2 vols. Boston, Bibliophile Society, 1905.

Shepard, Odell, ed. The Journals of Bronson Alcott. Boston, Little, Brown, 1938.

Sherwin, Oscar. "Prophet of Liberty: A Biography of Wendell Phillips." Unpublished doctoral dissertation, New York University, 1940.

Siebert, Wilbur H. "The Underground Railroad in Massachusetts," *Proceedings of the American Antiquarian Society,* XLV, Part 1 (April 1935), 25–100.

Smith, Herbert A. "The Early Forestry Movement in the United States," *Agricultural History*, XII (October 1938), 326–46.

Sumner, Charles. The Works of Charles Sumner. 15 vols. Boston, Lee and Shepard, 1872.

"Survey of the Coast of the United States," *Hunt's Merchants' Magazine*, XX (February 1849), 131–49.

Wagner, Vern. "The Lecture Lyceum and the Problem of Controversy," *Journal of the History of Ideas*, XV (January 1954), 119–35.

Wetherbee, Rebecca. "Memoir of Cyrus Hubbard," in *Memoirs of Members of the Social Circle in Concord, 2d Series, from 1795 to 1840*. Cambridge, Massachusetts, Riverside Press, 1888.

Whitford, Kathryn. "Thoreau and the Woodlots of Concord," *New England Quarterly*, XXIII (September 1950), 291–306.

Wood, James P. "Mr. Thoreau Writes a Book," *New Colophon*, I (October, 1948), 367–76.

Wright, Ellen. Elizur Wright's Appeals for the Middlesex Fells and the Forests, with a Sketch of What He Did for Both. Medford, Massachusetts, privately printed, 1904.

DATE DUE

WITHDRAWN